Angelic Reiki

Angelic Reiki

'The Healing for Our Time', Archangel Metatron

CHRISTINE CORE

BALBOA PRESS
A DIVISION OF HAY HOUSE

Copyright © 2011 by Christine Core.

All rights reserved. No part of this book may be used or reproduced by any means, graphic, electronic, or mechanical, including photocopying, recording, taping or by any information storage retrieval system without the written permission of the publisher except in the case of brief quotations embodied in critical articles and reviews.

Balboa Press books may be ordered through booksellers or by contacting:

Balboa Press
A Division of Hay House
1663 Liberty Drive
Bloomington, IN 47403
www.balboapress.com.au
1-(877) 407-4847

ISBN: 978-1-4525-0329-5 (sc)
ISBN: 978-1-4525-0331-8 (hc)
ISBN: 978-1-4525-0330-1 (e)

Library of Congress Control Number: 2011960689

Because of the dynamic nature of the Internet, any web addresses or links contained in this book may have changed since publication and may no longer be valid. The views expressed in this work are solely those of the author and do not necessarily reflect the views of the publisher, and the publisher hereby disclaims any responsibility for them.

The author of this book does not dispense medical advice or prescribe the use of any technique as a form of treatment for physical, emotional, or medical problems without the advice of a physician, either directly or indirectly. The intent of the author is only to offer information of a general nature to help you in your quest for emotional and spiritual well-being. In the event you use any of the information in this book for yourself, which is your constitutional right, the author and the publisher assume no responsibility for your actions.

Any people depicted in stock imagery provided by Thinkstock are models, and such images are being used for illustrative purposes only.
Certain stock imagery © Thinkstock.

Printed in the United States of America

Balboa Press rev. date: 11/28/2011

To Kevin Core,
my beloved husband who now graces us with
his loving presence as an aspect of the Archangel Yophiel.

The Great Invocation—(Short Version)

From the point of Light within the Mind of God
Let Light stream forth into the minds of men.
Let Light descend on Earth.

From the point of Love within the Heart of God
Let Love stream forth into the hearts of men.
May Christ return to Earth.

From the centre where the Will of God is known
Let purpose guide the little wills of men
The purpose which the masters know and serve.

From the center which we call the race of men
Let the Plan of Love and Light work out
And may it seal the door where evil dwells.
Let Light and Love and Power restore the Plan on Earth.

Words given by The Ascended Master Djwhal Khul to Alice Bailey. (Lucis Press)

Contents

Acknowledgements xiii
Introduction xv
Chapter 1:   Personal Stories 1
             My Story 1
             Kevin's Story 4
             Not a Normal Child. 5
             Nowhere Else to Go. 7
             The Birth of Angelic Reiki 8
             The Female Perspective 9
             Twin Flames. 11
Chapter 2:   The Time is Now 12
             The Reconnection 15
             A Message from The Archangel Metatron 16
             Why Is Angelic Reiki Here Now?. 17
             The Angelic Aspect of the Reiki Symbols. 19
             Angelic Reiki and other forms of Reiki and
                Healing 19
Chapter 3:   Insights and Revelations 23
             The Physical Body. 23
             The Etheric Body. 24

	Life	24
	Consciousness	25
	Attunements	26
	Reiki Symbols	26
	Raku	28
Chapter 4:	**Angels**	**31**
	A History of Angels	31
	Angels as Divine Design	34
	Angels As Archetypes	35
	The Archangel Michael	35
	The Healing Qualities of the Archangel Michael	36
	Meditation	37
Chapter 5:	**Getting to Know the Archangels**	**38**
	What Is in a Name?	40
	The Archangels of the Tree of Life	43
	Meditation to Connect to Your Sphere of Consciousness	51
	Meditation to Create a Deeper Connection to the Archangels through Colour	55
Chapter 6:	**Disease**	**58**
	The Truth?	58
	Where Do My Views of Disease Come From?	60
	Why Did Kevin Have Cancer?	60
	Spiritual Adages and Sayings	62
	Channelling from Djwhal on Disease	63
	The Gifts of Disease	64

Chapter 7:	Healing 69
	The Healer's Role in the Healing Process 74
	Angelic Reiki Healing 78
	An Angelic Reiki Healing Session. 79
	Follow-Up Appointments. 84
	Evaluating the healing 85
	The Bigger Picture 86
Chapter 8:	The Ascension Process. 88
	Channelling from the Elohim 9th June 2010 89
	The Symptoms of Ascension 92
	Physical Symptoms of the Ascension Process 94
	Angelic Reiki and Symptoms of Ascension. 108
Chapter 9:	Indigo Children and Adolescents 109
	Older Children and Adolescents. 110
Chapter 10:	Cleansing and Dedication of the Space 112
	Cleansing the Space 112
	The Dedication of the Space 113
	Our Spiritual Tools 117
	Magic. 121
Chapter 11:	Death and Dying. 123
	The Deathing Process 128
	The Long Death 128
	The Short Death. 129
	The Gift of Healing through Death 143
	The Seven Step Process for Healing through Death. 143
	Those Left Behind 146

Chapter 12: The Invocation of Angels for Specific Purposes....147

        The Gifts of Seventy-Two Angels.............149

Resources..161

Sources..163

About the Author..165

Acknowledgements

Throughout the whole of the writing of this book I have felt the presence of my Beloved late husband Kevin with me. It was his wish, right to the end to write this book and, my Love, you have. I am deeply grateful for this amazing support.

Here on earth my gratitude goes to Petra Mourtzoukou who put her own life on hold for three months in order to come and stay here in Egypt with me giving me constant help and support. Her devotion to Angelic Reiki continues to be invaluable. My gratitude also goes to Steve Minchin for his devoted hour of proof reading. Also my thanks and appreciation goes to Amandha Vollmer for her support with editing. These lovely people have given their time and skills freely in service and dedication to embracing as many people as possible in the arms of The Angelic Kingdom of Light. I am humbled and honoured by their support. Thank you and Bless you.

Introduction

I always wondered how it would happen, the start of this book. Kevin first promised to write this book nearly five years ago now, at the request our Angelic Reiki students who thirsted for more of his wealth of information and the beautiful, simple and pure spiritual principles that underpin Angelic Reiki. But on the physical plane, Kevin isn't here now. He left this incarnation on the 2nd of June 2009. The last three years our lives together have been dedicated to healing through cancer and it is that profound experience that has given me deeper insights into the disease and healing process. So I sit here in his office, his Angelic Reiki Master Crystal on the altar, to write the book that he never did in physicality.

Today, 22nd of August 2009, is probably the most poignant and hilarious day of my life. I have said 'I' am not here to write the book, but I'm not sure that is totally true. It will be interesting to see who does write this book. I awoke in our villa here in Luxor at 3.33 this morning and realised that the room was full of purple light. I got up feeling refreshed and wide awake and sensed a voice that said "It's now time to write the book."

Kevin had felt that it was very much part of his life's purpose to write this book and I'm sure he will have a special input. About two months before he died a dear friend of ours, Alex, came to visit. She told me later that she had asked him why he was hanging on and not allowing death to take its course. She asked, "Is it leaving Christine?" He had replied that it was but also he wanted to write the book. Well my Love we are writing it now.

This will inevitably be a book of many sources. Kevin has returned to his essence as an aspect of the Archangel Yophiel and will bring a radiant Angelic Love, but this will not be the only source from which this book is channelled. Archangel Metatron was the original guiding source of

Angelic Reiki and I am sure will be the main guiding Light. The Ascended Master Djwhal Khul will also be a potent and loving messenger.

Since its birth in the spring of 2002 Angelic Reiki has spread quickly and as I write it is represented in twenty-three different countries around the world.

This book is dedicated to Kevin Core, with great gratitude for his unwavering commitment and dedication to truth. It is also dedicated to all those who have spread this gift of the Wisdom and Love which is Angelic Reiki.

Chapter One
Personal Stories

My Story

Although this is part of the first chapters of this book it is the last one I write. To write a book is to share, not only the message and information but of oneself. I feel that in order to answer the questions *"What is Angelic Reiki* and *where did it come from?"* it is important for me to share something of Kevin's and my own story. It is reasonable for the reader to want to know something about the founders and channels. All of spiritual knowledge and wisdom is equally available to everyone. It is, though, our responsibility as human beings to receive theses Divine gifts and create something with them here on this Earth. We each follow our own *dharma*, life's purpose, in the way we collaborate with spirit. All of the ingredients that are brought together for a healing system are available to everyone. The way in which these are woven together depends upon the insights, wisdom and understandings of the weaver.

My family background was rather paradoxical and it is amazing for me to observe how this played out in the 'positive' and 'negative' experiences. It was deeply spiritual on one hand and on the other very challenging. My father experienced a spontaneous healing of chronic asthma in his early twenties and therefore gave me a belief in healing and of how the Will of the Divine governs everything. Even though this was in the 1940s and 50s there was an understanding of creating ones own reality. I can recall, at about the age of twelve and thirteen, engaging in deep philosophical discussions about the nature of God and creation. I did not receive any childhood vaccinations and have only once in my life taken any antibiotics and that was only for a few days. School was a nightmare. I was a dyslexic child before dyslexia was recognised. Reading was very difficult, writing

Christine Core

all back to front but I was enchanted by the patterns I could see in number and shape.

I qualified as a teacher, married and had two sons. It was then that the suppressed grief of the death of my mother when I was twenty and away at college caught up with me. Chronic insomnia and a whole range of minor ailments were affecting my life. I was doing yoga at this time, and one evening, I gave a lift home to someone who told me about homoeopathy. About ten months later, after a particular homoeopathic remedy, I woke one morning and had a profound knowing that I wanted to train as a professional homeopath. Interestingly enough this was in 1987 at the time of the Harmonic Convergence when many people of my generation experienced major changes in their lives. During the four years homoeopathic training I took short-term teaching contracts earning enough to qualify for a small mortgage which I used to purchase premises and create a centre for complementary and alternative therapies. It was at this point that my first marriage ended. I was to run the centre for the next nine years. During this time there were as many as twelve different practitioners at any one time working out of the centre. This brought the gift of introducing me to a wide range of healing modalities. I took the Masters attunement in Usui and Shamballa Reiki and study the Merkabah, offering these workshops at the centre.

In 1996 a massage therapist joined the healing centre but just stayed three months. During that time he did not see any client but kept popping in and out of the clinic. One day, when I was having problems with my new computer, he told me that he had a friend who was very spiritual and also had some expertise in the area of computers. He obviously thought I needed a spiritual person to help me with my computer! So Kevin, who was looking for a place to start his healing practice, came to the clinic ostensibly to help me with my computer. He joined my group of friends who met at my house to do meditations and share celebrations of the new moon, solstices and equinoxes. One day, I mentioned to him as he was leaving my home that I was doing a Merkabah workshop and asked if he interested. The ancient wisdom that underpins the teaching of the Merkabah is the creative principles that describe the Angelic Kingdom. We shared healing exchanges, joined the local circuit of spiritual speaker and started our own meditation groups. One day Kevin invited me to his house where we watched Diane Stein's video on Reiki. Just watching this video was to be a major initiation and weaving together of our energies. This took both of us many weeks to integrate.

In 2002 we were to go our separate ways our paths merging again in Kuala Lumpur some fifteen months later. I had felt that the phase of being a homeopath and running a healing centre had come to completion. I sold the clinic, rented out my home, packed a rucksack and bought an around the world air ticket.

My first adventure was whilst canoeing down the Wanganui River in New Zealand and connecting to a past life as a Maori healer. Five months later I was to receive an amazing initiations and activations from the Aborigine tradition at Uluru. A couple of months after that I found myself in the jungles of Borneo. I taught a couple of Shamballa Reiki workshops here one amazingly to a tribal village. A friend in Kalimantan, the main city in that area, had recommended he look after my passport whilst I travelled, so I arrived in the jungle town of Kabupaten Sanggau and was promptly arrested for not having any identification papers. The police offered to have an officer, who was flying in the next day, collect and bring my passport with him. At 4.00 in the morning I was awakened by the powerful presence of St. Germain with the message that I should try to prevent this as I would pay a large sum of money to retrieve my passport. I managed to contact my friend in Kalimantan and give him the message. Before leaving on this trip I had done a healing for the wife of a high-ranking police officer in the city and we managed to persuade him to vouch for me. I was finally free to travel. The Dayak people, who extend their ear lobes down to their shoulders, were the native peoples of the area. The 'Grand Mother' of a village about two hours up stream had been unwell since being flown to Jakarta as a cultural representative for an international gathering. On arrival in the village I was asked to do a healing for her; a wonderful honour and unique experience. The next week I caught a flight out of Borneo, met up with my son, (whom I hadn't seen for over a year) in Phnom Penh, Cambodia and set off on the next adventure. Thank you St. Germaine, for your intervention.

Kevin and I got married three times. The first was a Hindu union in Sri Lanka. The night before the ceremony Kevin and I had profound experiences. Kevin received an integration of the Divine Masculine and I the Divine Feminine. It was like a river of energy flowing down through all levels of reality bringing a conscious awareness of all beings that hold the masculine and feminine presence. This was the second initiation we received confirming that our relationship was not just about us. The work that we had to do and the reason we were together was to serve spirit through a merging of the Divine masculine and Divine feminine. We were legally married in the UK in 2007 which was flowed the next day by a 'Hand Fasting' ceremony shared with family, friends and the Angelic Reiki family. There is a short video on my web site www.angelicreikimagic.com.

Of course a significant experience in my life was being with Kevin through the time he had cancer and I mention significant aspects of this in later chapters.

Kevin's Story

Much of this book will be written from 'Balcony Moments'. Every morning as soon as we got up we would sit on the balcony of our bedroom which overlooks the verdant fields of the Nile Valley. It is a time of quiet and peace as the sun rises and Egypt awakens to the new day, the energy of new beginnings, the Archangel Raphael and the elements of Air. Air is mind, wisdom and inspiration. These energies used to come in very strongly as we sat sipping our morning drink. The whole of our life together was a time of exploration to understand the nature of spirit. It was at these times in the morning, as we talked and discussed our own insights, that we shared a time when spirit would reveal new levels of insight and inspiration.

Of course, even though Kevin is not in his physical body, this all still happens. So I share with you Kevin's life story as he shared it with me over the years we were together, with him still close to me, and inspired by this morning's 'Balcony Moments'.

First of all it is important for me to say that this is Kevin's life story as he told it to me. I am not making any medical claims or comments, and as always it is up to the reader's discernment, own wisdom and qualified advice as to what is right and true for them.

Kevin's Soul chose an extremely challenging life this time round. His life is a perfect example of how there is no correlation between how easily and smoothly one's life unfolds and how spiritually aware one is. There is a belief system which suggests that if one's life is easy and full of joy, Love, and light then one must be very spiritual. I don't believe this is a correlation one can make. When we come to an incarnation with the possibility of it being the last one in our rounds of 3-D experiences, the Soul collects together every remnant of the lessons we haven't learnt and presents them to us. If we have the courage to face such a lifetime, then the light we bring is truly magnificent; but just like any bright light it will find every crumb and speck that has not already been brought into balance. We have just got to look back in history to see how beautifully spiritual lives have rarely been easy ones.

When we are born we actually 'die' to the intimate knowledge we are a part of the Divine, we are beautiful and perfect, and that we are constantly in the arms of Divine Love. It doesn't have to be like this but it has been for the majority of people who have taken a sojourn on Earth over the last 2000 years. It can be very challenging when someone is born and does not die to the knowing of this truth, but all around them contrived to deny this truth.

This was Kevin's experience. He was born maintaining an intimate connection to spirit, feeling, sensing and hearing spirit all around him. His mother was an alcoholic who had denied all her intuition and spiritual gifts. Sensitive people often become alcoholics to numb the pain of not knowing. Even when Kevin was a tiny baby his mother was often not at home to care for him. She would lock Kevin in his bedroom so that he was 'safe', and beat and scolded him when he told her of the spirit presences that he could feel and hear around him. Kevin's connection to spirit became a great source of pain.

Not a Normal Child

There was nothing that would prevent him from being very different from other children. At the age of seven his intuition and sensitivity enabled him to write amazing stories. This perplexed his teachers as kids from poor backgrounds, without an educated family, were not expected to be able to write essays of that quality and insight.

At around the age of twelve he was not to be found playing football with the other boys. He told me he remembered finding the concept of competition strange and unappealing. He was to be found sat reading Greek mythology in the local library.

His social background created prejudice in terms of his educational aspirations in senior school and family attitudes believed he should not aspire to being more than a shop floor worker. He worked for most of his life in engineering. He wanted to be a teacher but his grandma told him that folk from their background didn't become teachers. Bless her, but how wrong she was.

Kevin told me that at the age of twenty-seven he went to bed one night and woke up the next morning a totally different person. It was a perplexing and rather disconcerting experience at the time. He gave up going out with the lads and instead took to reading the works of Schopenhauer, Gurta, Young and Nietzsche. What "freaked him out", (Kevin's expression) was that, without a proper education he totally understood the philosophy and concepts of these great writers.

Many factors in his life, as I am sure you can imagine, plus the nihilist philosophy of people like Nietzsche led him into a period in his life of profound depression. But he was still being intimately touched by Spirit. One of the times when he seriously tried to take his life was in fact a major turning point. He consumed alcohol and pills which to any medical opinion should have been '*successful*'! He told me how the following morning he awoke feeling perfectly okay but bewildered. Was this Divine intervention? I can only leave this to your own opinion. He then realised there was nothing that he could do to successfully end his life. So there was no point in trying. The state of depression was leading nowhere and by this time he was married and had a young son. No help he sought had been of any benefit. So finally he surrendered and did what spirit had been prompting him to do for years: meditate. He realized later this support was coming from the Ascended Master Djwhal Khul and Djwhal Khul had been with him all his life.

Angelic Reiki

Nowhere Else to Go

He had nowhere else to go so finally he followed the guidance of Djwhal Khul. Within six months his depression had gone. As this inner voice of this Master grew more prominent, he came to realise Djwhal Khul had in fact been with him all his life.

With this the next phase of his life began and he started to seek the company of people who were involved in spiritual work. They told him he was a healer, but Kevin never believed anything until he proved it to himself. He didn't believe it was Djwhal Khul who had been guiding him all his life until he proved to himself that messages from a particular essence or energy were always right. One day his son was unwell so with nothing to lose he tried healing. Of course it worked and very quickly his son was well again.

In 1992 Kevin was diagnosed with chronic bronchitis. He had been suffering from chest symptoms for the previous few winters and it had become particularly bad. The response of the medical practitioner was to advise him to consider giving up work as he expected the condition to worsen and that he should really take seriously the prospect of having early retirement. Kevin's response was to do self-healing. One year later a new job required him to have a full medical examination. Part of this was a chest X-ray. He enquired as to condition of his lungs. The doctor wondered why he was asking so Kevin explained that a year ago he had been diagnosed with chronic bronchitis. The doctor said that he could find no trace of the disease in the X-ray.

A new phase of his life began. He was working as an engineer during the day, getting up early each morning to do his meditation and going out each evening to fulfil healing requests. He also started reading books on spirituality but not the new writers of today. He studied western esoteric writings by Alice Bailey and Dion Fortune, Western mysticism and the Kabbalah and Eastern philosophy through the writings of Patanjali, Paramahansa Yogananda and studying the Bhagavadgita.

In 1995 Djwhal Khul prompted him to give up his day job and give over all his time to healing. Ascended Masters never tell us what to do; they simply plant an idea in our consciousness and it is totally up to us whether we follow the guidance. By this time, Kevin had three children and giving up one's day job is not an easy thing to do. But by now he was so confident of the guidance he had always been given by Spirit he followed the impulse. It was of course a challenging time and an opportunity for many lessons to be learnt, as it always is.

Our lives now started to weave together. In 1992 I had completed my professional training as a homoeopath and set up a healing centre on the outskirts of Bradford, in Yorkshire, England, the town where I had always lived. This is also where Kevin was born. We had gone to the same school and now we lived, unknowingly, only five minutes away from one another. I was having problems with the clinic computer and one of the therapists at the practice felt it was only right for a spiritually minded person to come and help. He obviously thought it needed to be a like-minded person who could assist me with the healing centre's computer. Kevin came to the clinic to sort out my computer and I offered him one of the consultation rooms for his healing practice. Now working at the same place we had the opportunity to exchanged healings and he joined a meditation groups at my home.

The Birth of Angelic Reiki

In 2001 I bought an around the world air ticket and travelled for the next fifteen months. Kevin continued with his healing but in 2002 was prompted by Djwhal Khul to start gathering certain pieces of information together. Kevin's decision to leave work had triggered within him a total commitment and trust in spirit. This abdication of personal needs and agendas facilitated his life to be now totally guided by the Angels and Masters. As the principles and structure of the new healing modality directed and facilitated totally by The Angelic Kingdom of Light unfolded, he did not know from day to day where he would go and what he would do. He tells a story of how one day after taking the children to school he was guided to go into the central library in Bradford. On arrival he was directed to go up to the third floor and turn right. About two-thirds of the way down the rows of shelves, on his left, he was directed to turn left and then pick up a book on the bottom shelf on the right hand side. This book was *A Dictionary of Angels* by Gustav Davidson. It was to provide the material for an attunement which allows the Reiki Symbols to be attuned to the Angelic vibration and thus to their original archetypal Angelic form. This is just one story of how for nearly a year Kevin's life was guided in order to bring together the material that was to be written down and named Angelic Reiki.

Kevin taught a number of workshops over the next few months and then a friend of his organised an Angelic Reiki workshop in Kuala Lumpur, Malaysia and one in Singapore. I was on my world travels and coincidentally was in Malaysia at the same time as Kevin. When he had left the UK on the flight to Kuala Lumpur and said his goodbyes he knew his life was to take another major turn. My journeys after Malaysia took me to Thailand and Japan, and after teaching a workshop in Japan I decided to return home to be with Kevin.

From then on we organized and taught the workshops together, and in 2005 we decided we needed to make our home in Luxor, Egypt, and live among the energy and inspiration of this great place.

The Female Perspective

Is everything birthed by men? Of course not, and they cannot do it on their own. It is the nature of the female principle to be unseen. The male input for creating a baby is visible and not hidden in any way. The baby in the mother's womb then goes through nine months of amazing change totally unseen.

At the start of workshops Kevin and I would tell something of the story of how Angelic Reiki came about. He would tell the story of how Djwhal Khul impulsed him to leave his job in engineering and to give his full time to healing and how he just followed the guidance in every moment as to when to meditate, where to go and which books to look at. We would tell the story of how he was guided to go to the local library and pick up the book '*A Dictionary of Angels*'. The actual channelling of the material that went into the workbooks and the structure and the philosophy of Angelic Reiki had been written down whilst I was away travelling and Kevin and I were not in a relationship at that time.

Christine Core

From 2007 I started teaching part of the workshops on my own because Kevin was experiencing pain in his throat, and during 2008 I was doing the majority of the workshops. When I was teaching on my own, I would tell the story of how Angelic Reiki came about but the students started asking me questions about the part that I have played. The presentation of the story up until then had been all about Kevin, all about the male energy.

Kevin had recognized and knew it was through me, the female energy, that the system was actually being grounded but there was no great story to tell. It was the asking of the question *"What was my part"* in a workshop space that allowed the bigger picture to be revealed and I had not realised the bigger picture myself. It is interesting to see how we had been acting out the male and female archetype. The male sexual organs are visible and external and there, in a way, for all to see. The female reproductive organs are deep within her body and the secrets of creation kept deep within her. There is a period of creation which is profound but hidden then after that time a birthing takes place and something independent is born.

Kevin and I had personally prepared ourselves for the conception of Angelic Reiki during our individual paths starting at the time of the Harmonic Convergence in 1987 and continuing throughout the 90's. Although our paths were walked separately, they were the same path. Both of us received Master attunements to Usui Reiki and Shamballa Reiki; we had studied and worked with the Merkabah, given up our normal jobs, and done a lot of personal work. Then in about 1997 after Kevin had come to work at my healing centre, he invited me to watch a video with him at his home by Barbara Stein on Usui Reiki. This turned out to be not just watching a video but a spiritual event where by our energies were merged. We both experienced unusual energetic changes for the following weeks. It was after that we exchanged healings and looking back, our life path had put in place a number of events that spiritually started to merge our energies.

In 2001 I decided to give up everything and go travelling. Astrologically I am water and I now see like the *Water Carrier* I was seeding my energy and imbibing the energies of many spiritual places around the world. It was whilst I was travelling that we *coincidentally* met in Kuala Lumpur, Malaysia. I had had an open ticket and was travelling wherever the impulse took me. Kevin and I had only exchanged the very occasional e-mail but one day I received a message saying that he would be in Malaysia to do a workshop organized by Colette from the UK and the timing of this was exactly when I was travelling through Malaysia. This was a three week period out of a fifteen month journey. Quite a coincidence! It was when we met in Kuala Lumpur that on the human level we fell in Love and recognized our deep connection. We had actually always lived only about 15 minutes away from one another and, although our age difference had meant we never met, we had gone to the same senior school. After visiting Thailand and Japan I cut my travelling short and returned to the UK to be with Kevin. It was very apparent that the purpose of our union was to balance the male and female so as to bring these two principles through our teaching and in the workshops.

It is now my life purpose to nurture Angelic Reiki through its adolescence and into full maturity.

Twin Flames

A number of well respected channels have said Kevin and I are Twin flames. A twin flame relationship is very challenging because its very nature means you are facing the perfect mirror. It starkly reveals anything that has not come into balance and has not been embraced unconditionally with Love. It is deeply searching and it is said that twin flames only come together to do spiritual work. As a relationship the tendency is to break apart because the other half is totally opposite to you in human, personality terms. I do resist spiritual drama and don't attach any great significance to whether Kevin and I were twin flames or not.

I know we came together on a deep spiritual level and the Love was absolute and the process of being together was a deep personal clearing for both of us.

This personal purification although challenging at the time, is one of the most profound gifts one can ever give another person. I am deeply grateful for the time we spent together and cherish every moment.

Chapter Two
THE TIME IS NOW

Not for 14,000 years has such a down-pouring of Divine Love been available to express itself through all those who work with the Angelic Kingdom of Light. And not for 14,000 years have so many people been turning to The Angelic Kingdom for healing and guidance. Now, the ability for the human race to experience the reconnection to the Angelic Realms is being reborn. It may be hard for us to imagine the feeling of merging, as co creator, with the Angelic Kingdom, but it is our Divine birthright and it is open to everyone. This has not been the case on Earth for a very long time but that time is returning.

"Angelic Reiki is the absolute joy of working hand in hand with The Angelic Kingdom of Light to bring one of the highest forms of healing to individuals, groups and the planet." (Quote from Kevin's guided information for the web-site).

We are all here on Earth now at a truly amazing time. In the great cycle of things our Solar System is coming to the completion of a 26,000 year cycle. Not only that; but our part of the galaxy is also coming to the end of a great cycle, and according to the Vedas and Indian tradition, we are also completing a 4.32 billion year cycle. This is the truth of what is happening to our planet and humanity at the moment. Events, cycles and the Divine Plan have been preparing for this time for Aeons. Every one of us on the Earth at this time has chosen to be here and is here for a purpose.

We Cannot See

It is difficult for us here on Earth to truly understand what a monumental and significant time this is. We see all around us people losing their jobs, the banking system and governments are wobbling and worldwide more wars and conflicts than have ever been known. But the truth is that all of this is the death throes of an age of darkness which is now coming to an end.

Give yourselves permission for a moment to daydream and imagine what would be the most beautiful and perfect way to live on this planet; seeing and appreciating only the beauty that there is on this Earth; knowing only support, Love and compassion from other human beings; living in supportive communities where everyone works together and life is happy and harmonious. It feels at the moment that this can only be in our imagination but actually this picture is a clue to the future.

The amazing changes happening on Earth are viewed by the Masters and the Angels with great awe and wonder. If we stop for a minute and realize that many, many beings in Spirit are looking our way amazed at the changes happening on Earth. They are also amazed at what humanity is now leaving behind and in great glee and excitement at the promise of truly a New Age.

The most powerful recent trigger for these changes was in 1987. It was called the Harmonic Convergence. Since then, literally, the vibration of this planet has changed. Every molecule and atom on this planet has changed its vibration. Our physical bodies have changed. The mitochondria within our cells and the chemistry of our cells are now more sensitive to light than they were prior to 1987. These changes are not just some idea or hope, they are facts, and they are true. We are evolving and mutating into beings that hold more light and with this we are moving into a time where Love and harmony will be the predominant experience of humanity on Earth.

Change happens gradually and it is a process. When we are in this process we cannot always see the bigger picture. The Angels and the Masters promise us this is true and that we are deeply in the process of moving into a new age, a golden age for humanity. This has always been the Divine Plan, this is the promise of the rainbow and it has no choice but to unfold. The Divine Plan is unfolding on Earth.

Christine Core

These changes mean we can feel and contact spiritual energy and Angels in a way not possible for thousands and thousands of years.

The most magnificent and amazing event that these changes have created is our ability to contact and reunite with The Angelic Kingdom of Light.

It is no coincidence that over the last few thousand years Angels have not been a part of daily life. It is not just the fact that books are being written about Angels and workshops facilitated to connect us to Angels that is creating a new awareness. If it had been possible to contact Angelic energy in the way we can now, it would have always been and they would have always been part of everyone's everyday life. But the truth is that the vibration on the planet prior to 1987 was not of a high enough frequency for us to contact the Angelic Kingdom in the way we can today.

This is cause for great celebration and great awe. It is no accident that the bookshelves are full of books about healing and Angels. It is simply a symptom, a demonstration, a manifestation of what is happening right now.

Just feel for a moment how blessed we are to be on the Earth at this time, a time where it is possible for us to actually commune and use all the gifts that The Angelic Kingdom can give us in our daily lives. It is actually difficult to comprehend the awesomeness of this, nevertheless it is true and it is where we are now.

Angelic Reiki offers and facilitates a deep and intimate relationship for everyone with The Angelic Kingdom of Light. A healing or attunement to Angelic Reiki, literally changes our DNA and every cell in our body; our consciousness and lightbody enabling us to more deeply attune ourselves and merge with the Angelic Kingdom.

For humanity to merge once again with the Angelic Kingdom is our destiny.

It is so long ago that we separated from the Divine in this way it is hard to remember what this beautiful relationship with the Angelic Kingdom can really mean. It means our daily lives can be guided and supported by the Angels. It means that our healing can be totally facilitated by the beauty and perfection of the Love of the Divine. This is what the Angelic Kingdom is; it is our connection to the *Perfection of the Divine*.

When I was a little girl I asked my Sunday school teacher 'What are Angels?' I still remember the answer. 'They are God's messengers to us.' This simple answer was true, the Angelic Kingdom are Gods messengers telling us we are always in their Love, we always are supported and we are always in contact with the Love of the Divine.

Imagine what it must be like to receive an attunement or a healing that deepens and facilitates an intimate knowing of this truth and a deeper unfolding of the Divine Love and Plan in our everyday lives. What greater healing could we ever receive than that which is totally and perfectly given to us by The Angelic Kingdom of Light?

The Reconnection

There is something very special in the way in which a connection is made with the Angelic Kingdom in Angelic Reiki.

Imagine you are going on holiday to the United States, Mexico, India or Australia, for example, and the attraction of that particular holiday is the opportunity to meet the indigenous people, to meet the American Indians or the Aborigines. The flight arrives at your destination and you are met by the tour guide and taken to your hotel. When you have settled in, your tour guide comes to pick you up in a minibus and take you to visit a local indigenous settlement. You are introduced to the people, whose language you do not speak, and you spend some time looking round the village and buying some of the local crafts. You then depart in a minibus and return to your hotel feeling you never really met those people, you didn't get to know them and no real contact was made. Imagine now a different scenario. You are met off the plane by a member of the local indigenous peoples. They take you to their village where you sit down in their home, drink tea and share a meal. You don't speak the language, but somehow joining them without an intermediary tour guide, sharing their food and playing with their children creates a connection beyond which your language could make. You were embraced by them in their home.

How would it feel for the Angels to welcome you into their Kingdom and for you to feel at home there and recognise a kinship? Only The Angelic Kingdom of Light can welcome you into their midst, can attune you to their energy and create an intimate relationship.

In Angelic Reiki this happens. The healer simply holds the space which allows the Angelic Kingdom to be communed with you, and in the workshops the teacher simply holds a space where the participant can meet The Angelic Kingdom of Light.

A Message from The Archangel Metatron

Channelled by Kevin Core

> 'At this time in the history of the Earth, the vibration in which the Earth exists has changed. All existence is based on vibration. There is at this time on the Earth the raising of the vibration of the Earth and this is allowing the higher vibration in which the Angelic Kingdom exists to now anchor upon the Earth.
>
> In truth, this means that your consciousness is raising its vibration. Your consciousness and the consciousness of the Angelic Kingdom are therefore meeting and co-joining and creating wonder upon the Earth. Angels are part of the Divine, and as such, the vibration of the Divine Mind flows through them. As your consciousness raises its vibration, you also are connecting now into the Divine Mind.
>
> The Angelic Kingdom is your guide to being the channels, the tools of the Hand of the Divine. Part of this knowledge, which we will give to you, is that system which is now known as Angelic Reiki. It is through this system you will be trained to carry the energy of the Divine Mind. You will feel the very thrill of the Life force flowing through you into your fellowmen. This life force has the power to change reality, as you know it. It is the blessed Breath of God.

By being the channel of this energy, you will allow yourselves, your consciousness, to merge with the Divine. This bringing together of human consciousness and Divine consciousness is that process which you now term Ascension. Those of you who are reading this have heard the call. We are calling to you all, to join with us, and to bring to the Earth the Divine Mind. The joy you feel in your heart is the very being of our existence. By being in this vibration, all your troubles and worries will disappear. The thought form humanity has held, which states that suffering must and does exist, is now fading away.

This knowledge will become a knowing for all of you. As this vibration anchors into your consciousness, you will see suffering has no foundation. Indeed, it is this vibration that will lift from everyone you seek to treat, that which they call illness; for illness cannot exist when joy is in the heart. This system, therefore, is transmitted to you now through that which you have known as Reiki. These symbols are doorways in consciousness and stretch through time and space. By opening these doorways the vibration, which we will channel to you, can treat all beings through time and space. We will reach into Earth's past and heal all memories of suffering. The Light of the Godhead shall anchor upon the Earth. The healing arts of the ancient times are re-awakening and will be given to you in this practice. Let the joy you feel in your hearts as you read these words guide you now into this vibration, which is embracing the Earth. The Angels have guided you to this place. They are embracing you now. Can you feel us? It is perfect that we are one. It is perfect that you are here. Perfection is the very life within you, and it is guiding you now. Open your hearts to the New Age, which is coming now. Let all doubt drop way. Let the highest vibration of Love anchor into your hearts. Start to breathe the whisper of Love's breath. Become the radiant child'.

Why Is Angelic Reiki Here Now?

Our ability to connect to this manifestation of the Divine has been shrouded from us for many thousands of years.

Our Earth and humanity have gone through a period of a perceived separation from the Divine. In the ancient texts of the Vedas this is known as the out-breath and in-breath of Brahma. In the out-breath of Brahma creation is created and goes out so far that it forgets who created it. We have been in a period of forgetting. This is not simply an idea; it actually changes the nature and vibration of us, the planet and everything around us.

Now, since The Harmonic Convergence in 1987, we have started on the return path back to the Divine. The path we follow is actually the same as the infinity sign with the centre being the source of creation of the out breath. Over the last 2,000 years, we reached the limit of that path away from the centre and are now on the return path home.

But this is not the whole story.

This process has happened more times than we can imagine and over such eons of time they are incomprehensible to us. At this time, now, on Earth, the impossible is happening. Something new is occurring and this is being triggered by the completion of three great cycles that have never come together before in our perception of creation.

This again is not something that is just spiritual theory or imagination. It has been recorded scientifically. We are literally mutating. Our physical bodies have chemically changed over the last twenty years enabling us to physically hold more light. You are becoming *'enlightened'* whether you know it or not.

These physical changes and the changes in our Lightbody mean that we can now merge with and work intimately with the expression of Divine light which we call the Angelic.

The process of merging with the Angels, which is the essence of Angelic Reiki, has only become possible over the last ten years. It's transformative potential is indescribable and the beauty, privilege and wonder at being able to merge back with the Angelic Kingdom is a gift and possibility for us all now.

The Angelic Aspect of the Reiki Symbols

The Reiki symbols were given to a group of lightworkers called 'The Inspirers' during the time of Atlantis. They were a special Divine gift to enable swift changes in consciousness. They are archetypes of consciousness and their names are sound codes that also affect consciousness.

When used with The Angelic Kingdoms of Light they take on an Angelic quality thus are tuning us to the Angelic vibration.

In Angelic Reiki the attunements to the symbols are given by an Angel that is specifically assigned to each person for this purpose. This means the vibration of the symbol and its qualities are not affected by the teacher. They are given in their perfect Divine Angelic purity.

Imagine what it must be like to be attuned to Divine Love by an Angel.

Kevin and I have often been asked to give a description of the energy and meaning of each of the symbols but actually this is not possible. These symbols are patterns of the Divine mind or pure Love consciousness. They are expressed throughout every aspect of creation, so there is a particular expression of the Divine mind or *'the intelligence of God'* on every dimension of creation. Within every dimension there are also sub-dimensions and actually it goes on like this infinitely. There are also the subatomic, molecular, genetic, mathematical, musical, paraphysical and superluminal aspects of each symbol. Creation is holographic and although we may intuitively get a feel for this, or feel the energy, our dear old human mind has no hope of describing or defining it.

Angelic Reiki and other forms of Reiki and Healing

The question "*What is the difference between Angelic Reiki and other forms of Reiki?*" is the most often asked question. All healing modalities have their place and they have all fulfilled their role. Everything always plays its perfect part in the Divine plan.

Everybody who has received an attunement into Angelic Reiki has given the feedback that it is different to anything else that they have experienced. Many people have come to Angelic Reiki as experienced healers in other modalities and have been in the field of spirituality for a long time.

The vibration of energy on the Earth and the energy that is available for us to contact, are connected. It would have not been possible for us to merge our consciousness with The Angelic Kingdom of Light a hundred years ago. This is possible now.

In order to utilise the highest potential in healing one needs to look at a healing system that is relevant today, one which embraces leading philosophy and utilises a method commensurate with the energies of today. The Archangel Metatron said that Angelic Reiki is the healing for our time. The Archangel Metatron gave this message to affirm that the vibration of Angelic Reiki does match the vibration that is here today. It also requires a philosophy and understanding which resonates with the new spiritual awareness.

The traditional way of working with Angels has been to perceive them as beings that stand around or with the healer as they work. Here Angels are perceived as something separate to the healer. Merging with the Angelic Kingdom means a uniting of consciousness and energy of the healer and the Angel. This is what is now possible. It is available to everyone and is the essence of Angelic Reiki.

There is always synchronicity of energy and needs.

This is a beautiful spiritual principle and demonstrates that the Divine Plan always gives us exactly what we need at any one time. We can easily forget that everything is part of the Divine plan when we are involved in the demands of everyday life. The material world seems so solid and everything around us is pulling us into the belief that this is what is real and important. Remarkably, even the Internet is part of the Divine plan. It is a physical representation of a web of information which we can log into. The Divine is also such a web. It resembles the Internet which reflects the closer connection we have today with a vast amount of knowledge. Where we are in consciousness is reflected in what is around us, and the evolution

Angelic Reiki

of consciousness has to be part of the Divine Plan. Even though we feel we are in control or playing a part in what is around us on a material level, the higher truth is that there only is the Divine Plan. We are part of that and it encompasses everything.

All of those involved in healing are, through their own dedicated, moving into a place where they can work with more subtle energies. In fact, everyone is now in touch with more subtle vibrations of spirit. Our consciousness is at a vibrational level where we can surrender to the Divine Will and give everything over to spirit. We can also totally give over the healing process to spirit and the Angels. With this realization comes the idea that there is nothing for the 'healer' to do. It is not the job of the 'healer' to 'heal' It is not the job of the 'healer' to clear this energy or malady. From this place where we give over the whole of the "healing" process to the Angelic Kingdom there is nothing for the healer to do. There is no decision as to which symbols to use, to chant the symbols, visualize or draw the symbols or move hand positions.

This creates freedom from the healer's personal opinions and assessments, and perceived abilities as a healer. It also releases the recipient from concern as to the energy with which the healer is working and thoughts about whether their situation has been fully understood.

Freedom from agendas and doubts

The 'healing' space for Angelic Reiki is one where the 'healer' lets go of all personal perceptions and sense of individual self, and through merging with the Angelic Kingdom create a space that is totally given over to the Angelic Kingdom. The 'healer' does not need to know whether the problem is because of a trauma in this lifetime or a past lifetime. We as individual human beings can never know the full picture. We simply do not have the resources to be able to perceive what the Divine and Angels can see.

In Angelic Reiki the 'healer' does not do anything but simply holds a space where the Angelic Presence will manifest.

In Angelic Reiki the teacher or Master does not do the attunements. The function of the teacher is to create a space where the Angels can manifest. An Angel merges its energy with each participant and facilitates the attunements. In this way everyone receives the pure vibration of the symbols and energies without human intervention. It is like an Angelic blessing and it changes every cell, molecule and atom and the consciousness of the recipient so that they are literally tuned into the Angelic vibration. The teacher does not take on the role as the person responsible for the attunements; they are there to simply facilitate the connection with the Angelic Kingdom. In a process whereby the Angelic Kingdom facilitates the attunements the 'Master Teacher' has to let go of all the egoic parts of self that wants to identify with a sense of teacher or Master. Angelic Reiki requires of its teachers innocence and humility, and an abdication of responsibility giving it over to the Angelic Kingdom. If energy is transmitted through a person's individual consciousness it is affected by that consciousness.

Another important principle of Angelic Reiki is the dedication of the space. Anywhere can be dedicated to a specific purpose and the dedication of spiritual places is an age-old practice. I will describe how this is done and how you can use it in many everyday situations to create a positive outcome in a later chapter. In the dedicating of the space the teacher or healer creates a bath of Angelic Love. For a healing this means that all negative energy is safely transmuted by the Angels, creating a protected and safe place for the healing. In a workshop it means that everything is under the guidance of the Angels and the whole of the process is in a bath of the Angelic vibration. In this space there is no need to be concerned about any negative energy which may be brought into the space. The light and the dark cannot coexist in the same place. It is impossible for anything of a lower vibration to be in that space. Everything is transmuted into love by The Angelic Kingdom of Light. This creates a beautiful and safe space.

Chapter Three
INSIGHTS AND REVELATIONS

I think it is important here to define some of the terms used in this book. I believe it is essential that there is a clear understanding of the words and concepts commonly used in spiritual writing. I feel it is a symptom of our disempowerment that, not only are words used without proper explanation, but that this has been acceptable to anyone involved in the spiritual world. A case in point is the word attunement. Many people have received attunements to Reiki and other energies but it is interesting to reflect on how many times this process has been adequately explained. I think it is perfectly reasonable to ask a workshop facilitator "What are you doing?" and "How does it work?" Someone who is giving you an attunement is changing your very consciousness and I feel it is reasonable to ask them to explain exactly what they are doing. I think we should be just as discerning as to who is giving us an attunement as to whom we would have sex with and I have to say that I think this has not always been the case. One of the reasons for explanations not being given is because the concepts are quite esoteric. I would like to start by describing reality and consciousness and how we work with it.

The Physical Body

From the simplest point of view this is a collection of elements and all of these can be found in a chemistry textbook which lists the periodic table. It is easy to find out what these are by looking at the ingredients listed on the side of any good vitamin and mineral supplement. The physical body is made of calcium, iron, magnesium, selenium, zinc, hydrogen and oxygen (water). There are also the vitamins. Vitamin C is ascorbic acid; vitamin E is a generic term for tocopherols and tocotrienols. (No I don't know what that means either), but a chemist would). The other component of the physical body is the nervous system which works on electrical impulses. At this level our body is a chemistry set.

There is also a tremendous amount of the physical world of which we are not aware. It is said that the comparison between what we see and hear and that which is not seen and heard is like a grain of sand to the height of the Empire State Building. The reality around us is difficult to understand because not only is it vast but it also has a holographic quality. Unfortunately the best reference that we have to understand this is the picture on a credit card, but simply being aware of this gives us a sense of awe. Although we cannot see nor hear the entire physical world it is possible to feel it and I will explain this in a later chapter.

The Etheric Body

Science is starting to recognise that there is an unseen aspect of the physical body. This is called the Etheric body. It is like an extremely fine electromagnetic cobweb that interweaves inside the entire body and around it. Strictly speaking this is not the aura. The Etheric body is just as much a part of the physical body as the bones and skin. It is rather like air as it is part of the physical world but we cannot see it, only feel it. It is the Etheric body that holds the patterns which creates the shape of all of the parts of the physical body. When a physical healing takes place it is actually the Etheric body that has been affected. In death it is the Etheric body that loses its connection to the physical body and thus life and consciousness no longer animates it. Without the two components, life and consciousness, the body is literally a pile of dust on the floor.

Life

Life is more easily understood if regarded as a synonym for the Divine. It is that force that courses throughout the universe. It causes cycles of creation and destruction and animates everything into form. It is constant and indestructible.

Consciousness

Consciousness is awareness of life. Consciousness is like a symphony around us. All the different tones, the high vibrations and the low vibrations merged together. The quieter and more still we are, the more of the great variety we pick up. All of the orchestra is playing and we can tune in to listening to one section more than another if we wish. There are different vibrations within this symphony of consciousness and these are called the dimensions. These are exactly the same as the keys on the piano. All the notes are divided into octaves and they can be played individually or all of them together. When high notes and low notes are played they merge together to create one unified sound. This is how the dimensions are. They can be thought of as different bands of awareness but they are not separate or in separate places.

Consciousness is a web of light and each dimension has a different pattern but they interweave and form a complex web around us.

This web of consciousness is who we really are. We are not the body; we are just borrowing and animating it with life through our conscious connection to It.

We are actually more than this symphony of consciousness. We are the conductor and creator, and the observer. We weave it at will and influence it by our every thought. It has a specific underlying pattern that is constant, but it is constantly being influenced by us.

If you were to connect to your own field of consciousness around the physical body which you inhabit at the moment, and then think of an elephant, there would actually be an elephant shaped thought pattern in your field of consciousness. Someone who is very clairvoyant would be able to see it. We often hear that thoughts are things and they absolutely are.

A friend of Kevin's, Edwin Courtenay, has amazing vision. After not seeing him for about five years I met Edwin just after Kevin's death at a spiritual conference in Athens. At first he didn't recognise me. It wasn't because I had physically changed over that time, it was because my consciousness had changed through my experiences with Kevin and living in Egypt. Edwin was looking at me as consciousness and not a physical being.

Attunements

Consciousness has an underlying pattern which is perfect and Divine and based on the vibration of Love. All of our thoughts and feelings affect our consciousness and distort it from its perfect Divine design. An attunement is the use of sound and/or a symbol to tune it back to being closer to its Divine perfection. The Angels and Reiki symbols are such Divine patterns that retune our consciousness. If the attunement is given by a person, it is coming through their consciousness and this will have an effect on that energy. This is why it is very important to be most discerning in choosing from whom you are willing to receive an attunement.

In Angelic Reiki the Master teacher does not do the attunements. The Angelic Kingdom facilitates the process. This means that the energy is untainted by a human consciousness. This is important and makes a significant difference. None of us are perfect and we all have our stuff that we are working through. Because the attunement is given by the Angels it is perfect and pure. It has its original perfect Divine design plus it holds an Angelic component.

Perfect consciousness is Love, but it is part of the human condition to not feel permanently united with the unconditional Love of the Divine. This means that our perfect pattern of consciousness has been distorted. A Reiki symbol holds the patterning of Divine perfection so when that is imprinted on our consciousness it reconfigures back closer to the original blueprint. This is how an attunement works. Just as you can place the thought pattern of an elephant in your consciousness a Reiki symbol can imprint it with the Divine.

Reiki Symbols

Kevin and I were often asked to write an explanation of all the Reiki symbols. Not only would this be more than one lifetime's work but it would actually be impossible. Every Reiki symbol has a holographic nature to it and an energy that resonates with every dimensional level. There are twelve dimensions and each of these has twelve sub-dimensions or sub-planes, and so on. Also each symbol has a subatomic, molecular, genetic, mathematical, musical, paraphysical and superluminal aspect to it. The conscious mind simply does not have references to be able to understand this. We can intuitively get a sense of the magic and profundity of receiving an attunement. It is a Divine gift that we have been given through the symbols that allows a re-attunement to the perfect Love of the Divine.

Most people do feel an attunement through Angelic Reiki to be a profound experience and many report that it totally changes their lives.

Raku

As I have said the multidimensional nature of the symbols makes it impossible for us to write down and describe their energy and meaning but I would like to give a brief introduction to one of them.

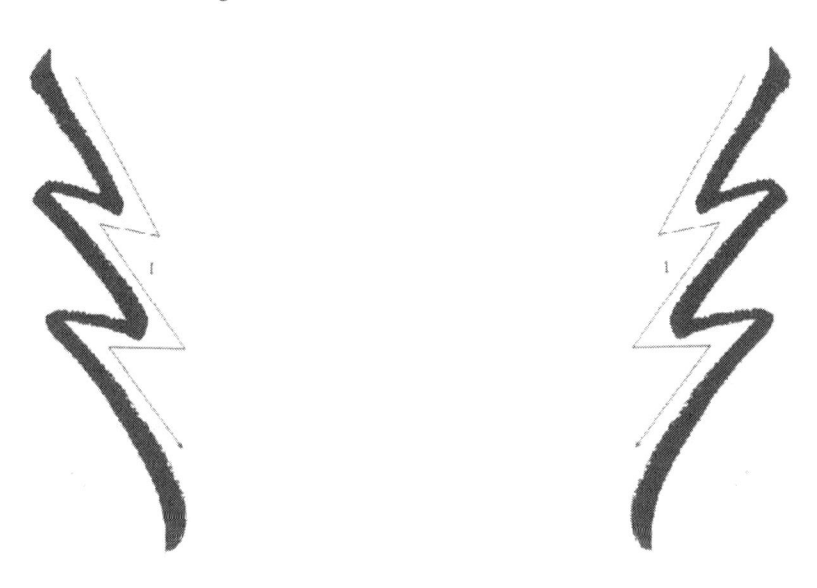

The Tree of Life

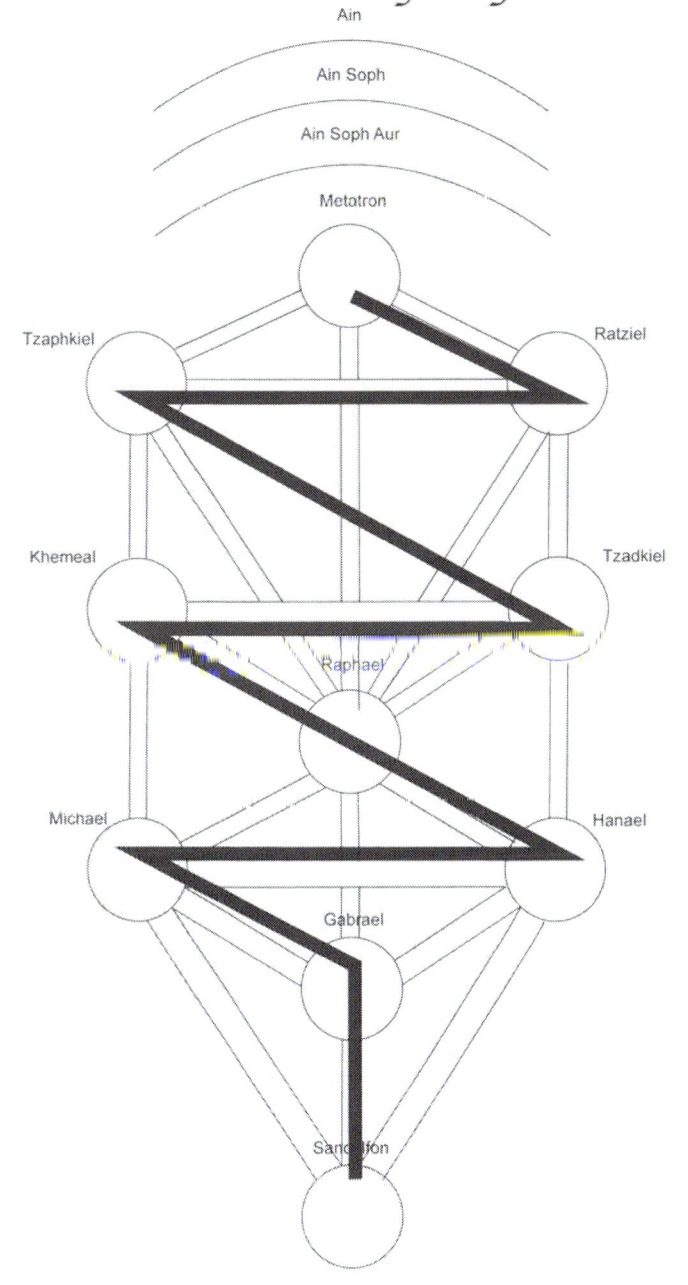

Ain

Ain Soph

Ain Soph Aur

Metatron

Tzaphkiel

Ratziel

Khemeal

Tzadkiel

Raphael

Michael

Hanael

Gabrael

Sandalfon

Christine Core

These pictures can say more than words. Raku, otherwise known as The Lightning Flash by those who study the Quabalah, (Kabbalah) is the creative energy connecting the Divine to the Earth and humanity. It connects the Archangel Metatron with the Archangel Sandalphon bringing the energy of creation to Earth. It connects together all the Archangels and creative principles, making it possible for us to experience that Divine connection. Also, in an attunement, it connects the Soul star, or Alpha chakra, with the Earth Star or Omega chakra. These are not chakras in the true sense of the word. They are energy centres with the Soul star being about ten cm above the Crown chakra and the Earth Star about ten cm below our feet. It represents unity and completion on every level.

Chapter Four
ANGELS

There is an amazing supreme intelligence which is the creator. This wondrous presence pulses out waves of energy gracefully weaving this web of life in infinite variety and form. It maps the cycles of galaxies and stars, spins the spirals of DNA and crystallizes the form of rocks and trees. It is an emanation of light and love and the web woven is of Divine design. The consciousness that holds this creative patterning is eternally perfect and in balance. It is the Angelic Kingdom of Light.

A look at our recorded history of Angels is an empowering revelation taking us on a journey from myth to fact.

A History of Angels

Today many people are connecting to Angels and they are becoming an important part of many people's lives. Pictures of Angels are seen everywhere in spiritual magazines, books and Angel card Tarot packs. Many current writers on Spiritual matters have popularised Angels in an amazing way. I'm sure that many people reading this have experienced Angels themselves or know of someone who works with that energy. I am also sure there are some of you reading this who feel you are missing out because you do not see Angels or you feel you have not experienced this special contact. I want to sweep away some of the myths and reveal to you that we are all intimately connected with Angels.

Throughout the whole of human history we have used images and symbols as a representation of something we cannot understand in any other way. For example, we would find it difficult to be constantly expressing our devotion and love for our partner, so we wear a ring to symbolise

Christine Core

our ongoing connection to that person. All big businesses use images or symbols to specifically try to convey a more powerful message than simply words could express. You may find it interesting to start to notice what the various symbols convey to you over and above the words that are used in advertising. For example your bank!!. Images and symbols are very powerful portrayers of messages. They have always been used to represent spiritual concepts we humans cannot totally understand. One of the most enduring symbols of spirit in many, many cultures has been the feather. American Indians use feathers in their ceremonial dress and the image of an eagle to represent spiritual wisdom.

The story goes back to ancient Egypt, some 10,000 years ago. One of the oldest symbols that uses the imagery of wings attached to a human form to represent a spiritual concept is the Goddess Maat. All the Egyptian Gods and Goddesses, known as the Neteru, represent a key archetype or principle. The Goddess Maat is depicted as a slim woman with outstretched wings which are at least as long as she is tall. She wears a single feather on her head. Maat is not the only Egyptian Neteru to be depicted with feathers or wings, but she is the one most linked to the story of the history of Angels.

All the wisdom and knowledge that underpins Western society came out of Egypt. Many influential figures and great teachers went to Egypt to learn Moses, Pythagoras, Plato, Jesus, and many more. The centres of learning were the temples, but in the year 3000 BC the key centre was the library at Alexandria. With the desecration of the temples and the destruction of the library in Alexandria immense knowledge was lost. In 48 BC, the library was partially destroyed by fire by Julius Caesar and in the third century AD the Roman Emperor Auielian caused significant further destruction during the wars at that time.

The ancient wisdom of the true spiritual significance of the imagery and symbology of feathers and wings was lost.

The story continues at the Treaty of Nicaea in 325 AD when the Roman Emperor Constantine, in order to keep his power, made a political decision to merge the Pagan and Christian beliefs of his empire into one religion: the Roman religion. The Emperor Constantine had a Pagan mother, but

Christianity was so powerfully sweeping his empire that he needed to embrace this new philosophy. At the Treaty of Nicaea all documents and writings that did not support the new religious philosophy were destroyed.

At the Council of Rome of 745, Pope St. Zachary, intending to clarify the church's teaching on the subject of Angels and curb a tendency towards angel worship, condemned obsession with angelic intervention and Angelolatry, but reaffirmed the approval of the practice of the reverence of Angels. This synod struck many Angels' names from the list of those eligible for veneration in the Church of Rome, including Uriel. Only the reverence of the Archangels mentioned in the recognized Catholic canon of scriptures, Michael, Gabriel and Raphael, remained licit.

Before 300 AD there is virtually no recorded reference in the Christian church to Angels, but by the 13th and 14th century great artists like Michelangelo and Raphael were using Angelic symbology in religious paintings. These pictures were of men with wings and, as we know, there had been a shift from the dominance of female energy to dominance of male energy in the last two thousand years.

In the New Age we have simply elaborated on the Christian image of an Angel. As this story illustrates, this image has come from a lack of knowledge of what an Angel really is. The information as to the true nature of Angels is part of the wisdom of Atlantis and was passed to the great civilisation of ancient Egypt.

In order to understand the truth behind the images and symbols that we use to represent Angels, we need to go back to find out what the ancient Egyptians were representing through their Goddess Maat.

The Goddess Maat symbolised *Cosmic Law*. So what is *Cosmic Law*? It is the *Laws* or *Archetypes of Creation*. They are the rules or designs that *God* or *The Divine Creator* used to create everything. Everything has to come from basic principles and the basic principle of this creation is three. This is represented in all philosophies, The Holy Trinity, The Father, Son and Holy Ghost, Isis, Osiris and Horus, and Shiva, Vishnu and Brahma. In a way *Cosmic Law* is very simple. It is number and the relationships of numbers which we represent as geometry. Unfortunately our education in mathematics has been very poor. We have not been taught the magic and poetry of number, so many of us shun away from mathematics and feel it is too complicated. It is not: it is very simple. The three main numbers that create the law for our universe are the, seven and twelve. Seven days of creation, twelve signs in the zodiac etc.

So if the true meaning of the image of wings is the creative principle of the universe, then Angels are a representation of the *law* of the creative energy of number and shape. The highest Archangel has always been recognized as the Archangel Metatron. The simplest geometry known is the sphere and the whole of this creation is based on the sphere. The Earth is round, we go round the Sun, we live through cycles and DNA is a spiral. It is all circular energy.

Many pictures of Angels today include a geometric shape, especially the Archangel Metatron. This is a true representation of what an Angel actually is rather than a picture of a human shape with wings.

Angels as Divine Design

There is great beauty in the order of the universe. One has only to look at the pictures of nebulae taken by NASA to see this beauty. And everything in creation follows a pattern. Our created world and universe is not only chaotic and haphazard but has rhythm, patterns and order.

This design ripples down through all levels. Archangel Metatron is the totality of all the principles of design and archetypes that have created our reality as we know it. Each Archangel is an aspect of that creative principle. Archangel Ratziel is the male principle of creation and the Archangel Zaphkiel the female principle. There are many aspects to the expression of each Archangel and these are called Angels. A group of Angels connected to a specific Archangel is known as an '*Order of Angels*'. We can see the same patterning in everyday life.

Angels As Archetypes.

The most accurate way to understand the nature of an Angel is to see them as an archetype. The dictionary definition of an archetype is "something that serves as the model or pattern for other things of the same type". Angels are the pattern of the Divine's creation. Everything is created by '*God*' and according to the stories of creation, we are in this likeness. When teaching I often use a sphere to illustrate the concept of an archetype. As an idea it is boundless and infinitely everywhere. If I wanted to make a football, a round bouquet of roses or a cannon ball I would first have to have the concept of something round. However frequently I or anyone else wanted to use the idea of round it would never be depleted and it would be always available to anyone else to also use. It is simply a concept or idea which follows particular rules. If I wanted to make millions of footballs this would not deplete the infinite potential to make something round. The concept or archetype of round or sphere also does not have an opinion or agenda. It is totally unconditional. It doesn't care whether I am going to use the archetype of sphere to make footballs for fun or cannon balls for war. It doesn't care if I am a good person or a bad person, how I am feeling emotionally or if I am thinking loving thoughts. I can use the creative model of sphere freely.

All Angels and Archangels are archetypes and are absolutely available, without limit for everyone who wishes to invoke their energy.

What a beautiful concept to know that, however you are feeling and however you might view yourself, The Angelic Kingdoms of Light are yours to work with unconditionally. You do not need to believe that you are good, spiritual or full of love before you can feel the Divine presence that is an Angel. There is nothing and no one that is not touched by the Divine pattern of Love which is the Angelic Kingdom and we are feeling this connection more and more.

The Archangel Michael

The Archangel Michael is one of the most well known and is therefore a good example to use in understanding the essence of Angelic energy.

Because of the history of Angels and their depiction as a human shape with wings, we have become accustomed to the idea of Michael as the name of this being. The *'name'* of an Angel is much more than simply a name. It represents and expresses the essence of that Angel. One of the reasons why poetry is so expressive, conjuring up the feelings, images and message which the poet wished to convey is because the words used have the sound and feeling of what is being described. The word *bowl* sounds round and the word *stick* sounds thin and sharp. In fact everybody's name holds the essence and rhythm of that person.

In the same way the name *Michael* is not simply the name of an Angel. The very word has a rhythm and quality which represents the essence of that Angel. Unfortunately we do not often use the correct pronunciation, which would more accurately be *'mm-EE-kII-eLL'*. An Angelic name is a sound formula that creates a specific vibration and energy. You might like to sound out loud *'mm-EE-kII-eLL'* three times knowing that you are invoking that Angelic vibration and feel what it feels like. That feeling is the essence of the Archangel Michael and through feeling the nature of this Angel it can be experienced in a deeper and truer way.

The essence or archetype of the Archangel Michael is the destructive and rebirthing aspect of the feminine. Another symbol of this energy would be late autumn through to early spring. In late autumn, the cycle of the previous year is coming to an end. All the leaves have fallen off the trees and the grass is not growing any more. Then there is a time of stillness through the cold weather and rains when all the leaves from the trees are broken down and become part of the soil again. In early spring, new shoots grow and there is a new beginning.

The Archangel Michael is often associated with transformation and the cutting of ties but, if experienced as an archetype, a deeper understanding of the essence of this aspect of Divine creation can be seen.

The Healing Qualities of the Archangel Michael

If we perceive Archangel Michael as something separate that comes to us to do a job we are limiting the transformative potential of this particular aspect of the Divine.

What would it feel like for that Divine principle that is completion, stillness and a new beginning through love to totally infuse every cell, molecule and atom of your being and to rebuild your physical, emotional and mental bodies according to this Divine blueprint? It isn't something that could ever go away. It is an infusing and merging of this Divine principle with everything that you are. In that moment you become the Archangel Michael.

Every time this process of letting go and new beginnings occurs in someone's life it is the manifestation of the Divine, that Divine principle that is the Archangel Michael.

Meditation

I invite you to close your eyes and take two deep breaths with the intention of letting go on the out-breath of any doubts you may have about feeling an Angelic presence. Sound the name *Michael* three times. The sound is *'mm-EE-KII—ell'*. Hold the intention for this sound to vibrate the whole space around you, you and every cell molecule and atom of your body. Let the sound, sound within you as well as around you and feel the vibration, the presence of the Archangel Michael. The feeling may be subtle or strong, but I can assure you that there will be a change in the vibration of yourself and your room. Imagine that you can actually breathe this energy. Let it fill your entire body. Sit in the energy breathing it, becoming it as long as you wish.

Chapter Five
GETTING TO KNOW THE ARCHANGELS

The information that we have of about Angels today is literally a hodgepodge of information passed down through a number of different traditions. I believe that about 5,000 BC there was a unified concept of Angels out of which our present day ideas have grown, but it has followed many roots: some through Egypt, some through Greece and others were nurtured in Babylonia (now Iraq). Gustav Davidson in his introduction to the book '*A Dictionary of Angels*' describes beautifully his dilemma and challenges in gleaning together information about Angels. Descriptions of Angels are to be found in New and Old Testaments of the Christian Bible, Kabbalistic writings, Jewish mysticism, Gnostic writings and in the Koran. Much of this information was translated by scribes from language to language and of course represented their interpretation. For example Gustav Davidson found nine quite different variations on the name for Archangel Uriel, most from Babylon. One of the most consistent and best preserved lineages of information about the nature of Angels is to be found in the Kabbalah. The Tree of Life is one of the models from this tradition that maps creation and consciousness. The Tree of Life has ten Sephiroth or circles, these and the twenty-two paths between the Sephiroth describe archetypes in a similar way to tarot cards. Each of these Sephiroth has an Archangel and a group of Angels associated with it. It is therefore through this tradition that we can get a feeling for the essence of each of the main Archangels.

The Tree of Life

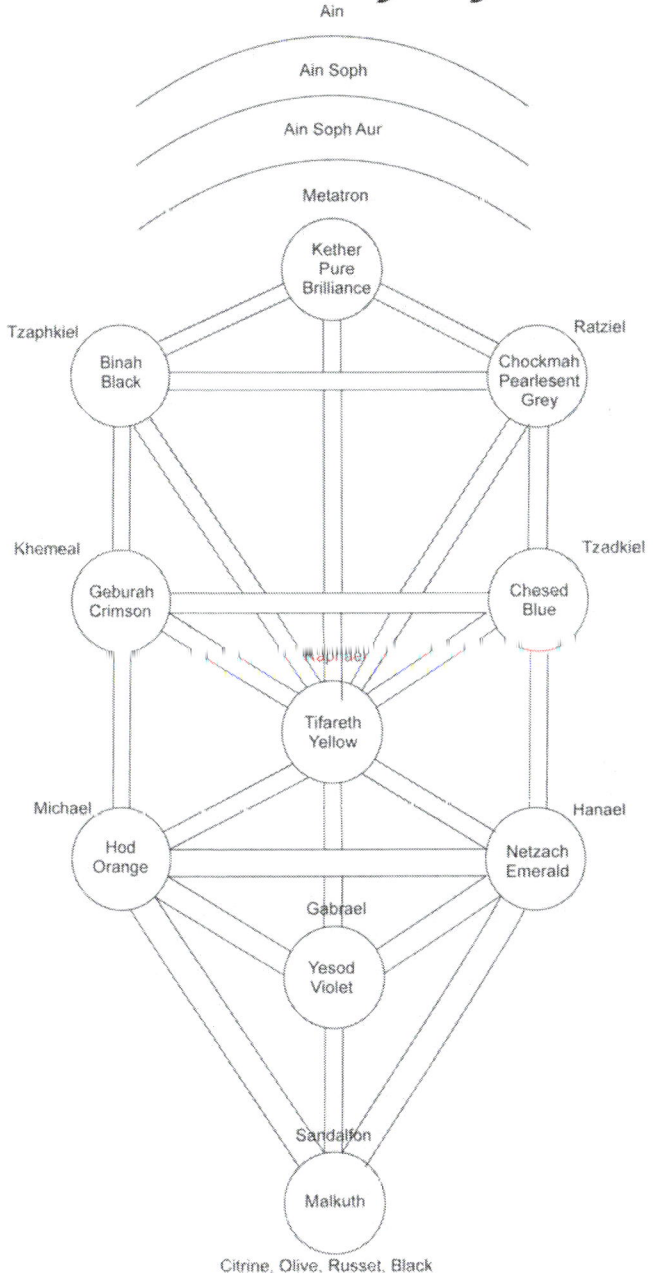

Ain

Ain Soph

Ain Soph Aur

Metatron

- Kether — Pure Brilliance
- Tzaphkiel — Binah — Black
- Ratziel — Chockmah — Pearlesent Grey
- Khemeal — Geburah — Crimson
- Tzadkiel — Chesed — Blue
- Raphael — Tifareth — Yellow
- Michael — Hod — Orange
- Hanael — Netzach — Emerald
- Gabrael — Yesod — Violet
- Sandalfon — Malkuth — Citrine, Olive, Russet, Black

What Is in a Name?

As I have mentioned in a previous part of this chapter Angelic names are creative codes or formula. To understand all of this requires a deep investigation into the languages of ancient Hebrew and Greek. That is where to look if you want to know the full meanings of the energy of these *names*. It is a lifetime's study but the table below gives an introduction to the root of one of the names, Michael.

All Angel names can be looked at in a similar way.

Letter	Sound	Numerical Value	Symbol	Meaning
M	Mem	40	Water	From, of, since
I	Zayin	7	Sword	Cut in two
CH	Ches	8	Fence	Enigma
A & E	Alph	1	Ox	Creative power of nature
L	Lemed	30	Ox Whip	Balance Justice

Some languages are sacred. The main purpose of many languages of indigenous people is for ceremonies, not every day communication. In the West we have lost a sacred relationship with our language and indeed the main languages of the West have lost their sacredness. Perhaps the most sacred language today is Sanskrit which is used only for prayer and never mundane communication. When a language is kept sacred the energy of the words is preserved and not polluted by everyday use. In ancient Hebrew the power of the words was known to be so great that they were kept secret only to be used by priests and initiates. The written words never included the vowels because they knew that the power was in the vowel. This meant that only those who have been educated into the wisdom of the sacred teachings could speak or write the sacred names.

One of the biggest pollutants on the planet at the moment is the noise made by people in casual conversation. You may have noticed that the more you get into spiritual work the less you have to say and that meaningless gossip is no longer of interest. My first husband and I were very much part of the professional business world and we used to host dinner parties quite regularly. I used to enjoy dinner conversations, but then one day I found that I had absolutely nothing to say. The subjects that were talked about suddenly seemed trite and had no interest. Casual conversation is mostly used to whip up the energy of life's dramas. Not only is it wasted noise but it actually locks us energetically into the drama and fuels it. As I became less interested in the soap opera of life I became disinterested in normal conversation. The aborigines believe that our voices should only be used for sacred ceremonies, songs and celebration. I actually believe that if the world was silent for three minutes, it would ascend.

In the diagram you can see that in Hebrew each letter has a full sound, a numerical value, quality or symbol, and a meaning. The numerical value of the angelic name Michael is eighty-six, which reduces to fourteen and then down to five. (This is done by simply adding the numbers together). There are many interpretations of the meaning of the number five and every tradition has its own ideas. There are some fundamental unchanging truths though. The number five creates the pentagram, which in spite of its misrepresentation, is based totally on the energy of love. The rose has five pointed leaves. It is the love of the Archangel Michael which brings forgiveness and new beginnings. The symbol for each letter in the name Michael gives us water, sword, friends, ox and ox whip. The possible interpretation of this could be that by cutting the attachment to the emotions we create boundaries that bring strength and we can leave the past behind. The meaning of each letter could be put together as saying that from putting away the past we can find hidden meaning that can being creative power and new balance.

Even through this very simple way of looking at the origins of the name Michael we can get a deeper understanding of the nature and essence of this Archangel.

We have just looked at a way of gaining a deeper understanding of Angelic energy through information and intellect. Another, perhaps easier and truer way is through *feeling* the energy and an understanding of what the American Indians call *The Medicine*. This is the essential (essence-tial) qualities of something: its nature, gifts and spiritual qualities. This of course includes Angels.

A good way to connect to these Archangels is to feel that essence as you read the corresponding energies. Ask yourself "What would it feel like to be crimson red, a member of the *Order of Angels* known as the Seraphim, a Warrior / Creator with great courage. This is the Archangel Chamael.

The following is a list of the qualities of all of the ten Archangels of the Tree of Life starting with the one at the top: The Archangel Metatron.

The Archangels of the Tree of Life

Archangel Metatron.

Archangel Metatron is the Archangel that is the first spark of creation and holds within its being-ness all the other Archangels and Angels. It is the primal source of all. Perfect and complete. It is not male or female but holds all potential for creation as a manifest expression of the Creator.

The colour is pure brilliance, beyond colour.
The sound of presence is El Shadi.
The power name is Ehieh.
The meaning of the word Metatron is 'Beyond the Matrix'.
The group expression or Order of Angels is the Chayoth Ha Qadesh.
The spiritual quality is union with source.
The Earthly quality is completion of a major task.
The Stone is Diamond.
The animal correspondence is hawk and swan.

Pictures of the Archangel Metatron often depict a geometric design in the background. This is commonly known as *Metatron's Cube* but the cube is only one small part of it. The pattern is generated by another pattern which is called the *Flower of Life*. This is thirteen overlapping circles. Examples can be found all over the world: Abydos Temple Egypt, on the side of a pyramid in Tibet and under the feet of the lions in Tiananmen Square China. It is a universal pattern that describes the design of creation. When the centres of the thirteen touching circles are joined together *Metatron's Cube* is created; the Divine Design of Creation.

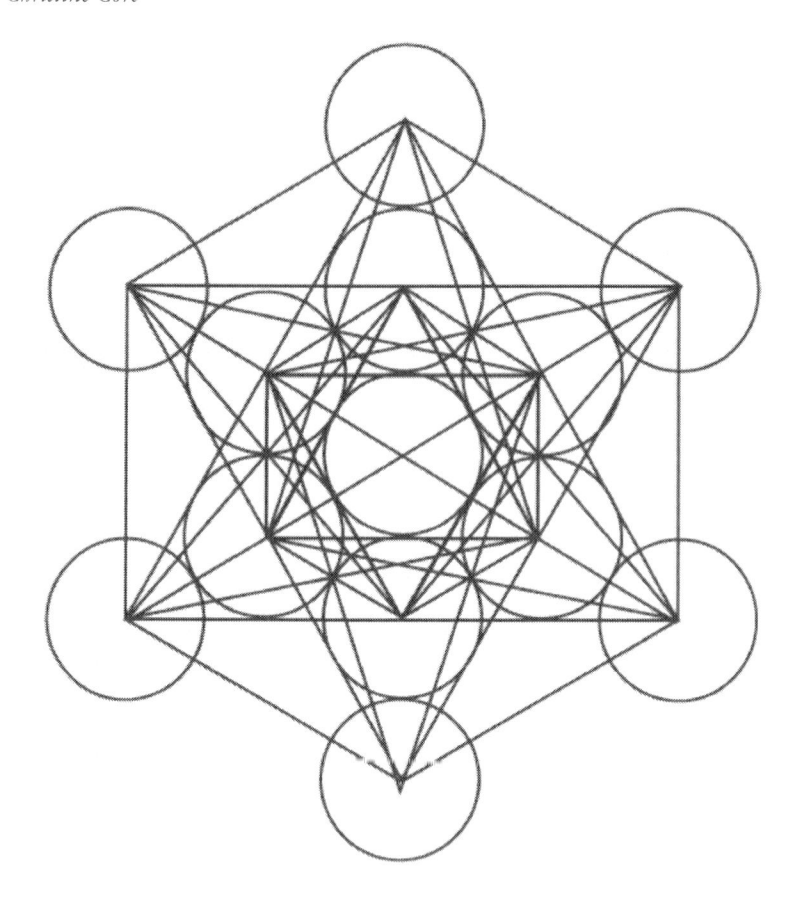

This is the essence of Archangel Metatron, but you have to imagine it as if in infinite motion generating vortexes, spirals and spheres of creative energy, spinning simultaneously in three directions at the speed of Light and Love. We cannot really visualise this but we can get a sense of the awesome creative potential.

Archangel Ratziel (Raziel)

Archangel Ratziel is the thrust and wisdom needed to create. Nothing is actually in manifestation but Archangel Ratziel is the will of the Divine in motion; just in motion; the impulse; the desire to create. It holds all the wisdom keys for creation. It is pure male energy, the infinite potential to create, but *just* that.

The colour is pearlescent grey.
The power name is Yehveh
The group expression or *Order of Angels* is Auphanim.
The spiritual quality is Wisdom of the Father.
The Earthly quality is Devotion.
The stone is Star Ruby.
The animal correspondence is Man.

Archangel Zaphkiel

The Archangel Zaphkiel is the infinite womb of the feminine principle. It is deep and boundless and like a black hole draws everything to itself as potential for creation. It is infinite and formless yet pregnant with the desire of the Divine to receive the male trigger to create. The Archangel Zaphkiel receives the full impulse of the Divine to create and holds it unto herself to ripen for birthing. It also embraces the archetypes of the Goddesses Isis, Shakhty and Kwan Yin.

The colour is deep eternal velvet black.
The power name is Yahveh Elohim.
The group expression or *Order of Angels* is the Aralim.
The spiritual quality is Infinite Female Womb.
The Earthly quality is silence.
The planet Saturn.
The stone is Pearl.
The animal correspondence is Woman.

The Archangel Zadkiel (Tzadkiel)

The Archangel Zadkiel receives the impulse from the triad of Archangel Metatron, Archangel Ratziel and Archangel Zaphkiel and holds the highest level of the Divine as it takes form. It is Love in action that holds and fosters the creation. It is male in essence, the Father holding the baby immediately after birth.

The colour is radiant royal blue.
The power name is EL.
The group expression or *Order of Angels* is The Chasmalim.

The spiritual quality is Benevolent Order.
The Earthly quality is Obedience.
The planet Jupiter.
The stone is Amethyst.
The animal correspondence is Unicorn.

The Unicorn is often seen in meditations as a symbol of new creations and new beginnings.

The Archangel Chamael (Chamuel, Khamuel)

The Archangel Chamael is the awe and power of creation. That creation, though, also destroys what was already there in order to bring in the new. The energy of this Archangel is truly awesome in its might and Power. It is akin to the powerful experience of giving birth. Chamael is feminine in essence but also has the energy of Mars and war, Boudicca and Athena.

The colour is crimson red.
The power name is Elohim Gibor.
The group expression or *Order of Angels* is The Seraphim.
The spiritual quality is Warrior / Creator.
The Earthly quality is Courage.
The planet Mars.
The stone is Ruby.
The animal correspondence is Basilisk.

The Basilisk is the legendary king of the serpents that could kill with a single glance. It is woven into *Harry Potter and the Philosopher's Stone*.

The Archangel Raphael

The essence of the Archangel Raphael is the life-giving rays of the Sun. As a sustainer of life, Raphael has always been considered the Angel of Healing. It brings everything into equilibrium, finding the still balance that can express the beauty of life to the maximum. The light of the sun illuminates anything that has been lurking in the dark bringing clarity and a harmonious expression of life. The glory and expression of Life.

The colour is iridescent pale yellow.
The power name is Yahvenh Eloah Va Daath
The group expression or *Order of Angels* is the Malachim.
The spiritual quality is Creation of Life through the Radiant Sun.
The Earthly quality is Service, Healing and Devotion.
The planet the Sun.
The stone is Topaz and Yellow Diamond.
The animal correspondence is Lion and Phoenix.

The Archangel Haniel (Aniel, Hanael)

The Archangel Haniel is a celebration of the multi-facetedness of creation. Like light divided into the colours of the rainbow it is the expression of the Divine Love that flows through poetry, music, ritual and celebrations. It is like the marriage of everything that has gone before preparing to birth the design in the material plane. It is that knowledge that life is in everything seeking to express itself.

The colour is emerald green.
The power name is Yahveh Tzabaoth.
The group expression or *Order of Angels* is The Elohim.
The spiritual quality is the Expression of Love.
The Earthly quality is Selflessness.
The planet Venus.
The Stone is Emerald.
The animal correspondence is Lynx.

The Archangel Michael

In none of the traditional sources is the Archangel Michael described as *a protector*. I believe this is a misunderstanding of the energy of this Archangel. The concept of protection brings the idea of separation and that there is some evil out there from which we need protecting. For me this is not the case. All is part of the creation of the Divine. My little cliché is that creation did not write any exclusion clauses. It is usually our shadow of which we are afraid.

Christine Core

The Archangel Michael was often painted by artists such as Raphael (Raffaello Sanzio da Urbino), Guida Reni, and Gonzalo Perez during the Renaissance or 'Golden Age' of 15th century Europe. The paintings show him with a sword slaying some evil being. A correlation with George and Dragon is also often made. This represents the slaying of our own daemons, overcoming through love of anything that brings up fear or a part of ourselves that we do not love. The Archangel Michael holds the energy of transmutation, not separation.

The Archangel Michael has always been one of the most popular Archangels, but this is an accident of history. In Christian, Jewish and Islamic tradition this energy is regarded as the greatest of Angels. The fact that the slaying of our own dark allows us to see the light of the Divine gave this Archangel the reputation that is close to *God*.

As you may have noticed I have not used the word '*he*'. The Archangel Michael is on the feminine side of the Tree of Life and is also traditionally associated with the energy of Shekinah the Divine Feminine. It is through motherly love that we can face out fears overcome/transmute them and move on.

It is also interesting that the traditional colour for the Archangel Michael is orange. Orange is the colour of the robes of the Tibetan Buddhists and Buddhism is one of the traditions, like Egypt, that has held the true wisdom about death seeing it as a rebirth; the transmuting of one state to bring about the next. Also it is said that an orange light in the room helps a dying person to move more gracefully through the process.

The Archangel Michael is the energy of glory, splendour and great brilliance. It is the light which shines in the darkness to transmute everything into its light and create new beginnings. The Archangel Michael is the process of making possible the expression on Earth of the Divine Light.

The colour is radiant orange.
The power name is Elohim Tzabaoith.
The group expression or *Order of Angels* is the Beni Elohim.
The spiritual quality is New Beginnings and Transformation through Love.
The Earthly quality is Truthfulness.

The planet Mercury.
The stone is Opal.
The animal correspondence is Jackal and Twin Serpents.

The Archangel Gabriel

Most Angelic names come from their original energy to us through the Christian / Judeo traditions, but for Archangel Gabriel it is not that straightforward. This Angel has played a significant role in many religions and philosophies. In Islam this Angel dictated the Koran to Mohammed, in Jewish legend destroyed Sodom and Gommorah, for Christians gave Mary the baby Jesus (Matthew 1:20; Luke 1:26) and guided Joan of Arc. The name actually comes out of Babylonia during the reign of Nebuchadnezzar its king in 600BC.

On the Tree of Life it is through The Archangel Gabriel that all the creative energies flow and are reflected downwards, before being grounded through the Archangel Sandalphon. The Archangel Michael has transmuted all energies that veil the light of the Divine to enable a rebirthing of something new. This process is done through the Archangel Gabriel. But this downw pouring of creative energy needs mind, building with it whatever it projects. This is also therefore the level of illusion where everything is a reflection and not the real thing.

This level of consciousness is associated with water, emotions and the astral plane.

The gift of the Archangel Gabriel is discernment allowing us to see emotionally triggered projection and what is a creation from the Divine.

Archangel Gabriel guides *souls* to connect to their physical bodies.

The colour is rich royal violet.
The power name is Shaddi El Chai.
The group expression or *Order of Angels* is The Cherubim.
The spiritual quality is the Potential for Creation on the Physical Plane.
The Earthly quality is Independence.

The stone is all colours of Quartz.
The animal correspondence is Elephant, Tortoise, Toad.

The Archangel Sandalphon

The root of this name is found more in Greek than Hebrew. The closest translation is "co-brother". The Archangel Sandalphon is often referred to as the twin brother of Metatron and this is where the name comes from.

The Archangel Sandalphon is the Angel of the manifested creation of the Divine. Our Earth, our bodies and all around us is as much a part of *God's* creation as anything else. There is no hierarchy of *Divineness*. It is us who have projected better or *holier* onto the idea of higher dimensions. All of creation is vibrating energy. To think of the higher dimensions as more Divine in some way is as untrue as to say that higher notes on a piano are more Divine than low notes. This assumption that higher means better is the illusion which the Archangel Sandalphon wipes away. This is the Angel which shows us that Heaven is here on Earth. It is up to us to embrace this Divine truth.

The realm of Archangel Sandalphon is known as 'The Kingdom', 'God's Kingdom'. This term is to be found in both Judaic and Christian texts.

The colour is citrine, olive, russet and black.
The power name is Adonai Ha Aretz
The group expression or *Order of Angels* is The Ahim.
The spiritual quality is Abundance of Earthly Manifestation.
The Earthly quality is Discrimination.
The stone is clear Quartz.
The animal correspondence is Sphinx, Geb, Pan.

Information helps us get a more accurate understanding of the nature of angelic energy. Another way is to feel and experience this energy. Since a specific change on 11th November 2005 (11/11/2005 {11+11+2+5=11}), our ability to feel energy has significantly increased. As well as the physical, emotional and mental part of ourselves, we are also pure consciousness. In fact this is really all that we are. Our consciousness is like a sphere of awareness around us. In this sphere is every level of our consciousness and it is multi-dimensional. It is in our consciousness that we can most closely perceive the nature of angelic energy. Usually we perceive the reality around us through our senses of seeing, feeling, smelling and hearing. We can also use higher aspects of these abilities in order to understand and get to know the nature of our own consciousness. Our five senses do have the same abilities on other dimensional levels. It is difficult for one mind to understand this and this information can only be picked up on the subtle levels. Also some of our senses are easy-to-use on these higher vibrational levels. Many people see colours and can pick up energetic changes through the colours they see. It is not difficult to sense the Archangel Raphael through its colour yellow. This colour really helps us get a sense of the qualities of this Archangel, but you will probably find it much more difficult if you were asked what Archangel Raphael smelt like. In order to start using our other senses to understand the qualities of our consciousness and Angels, the conscious mind needs to be tricked into letting this information through. It firmly believes that it is not possible to smell the Archangel Raphael. To trick the conscious mind so this information can be allowed in, close your eyes and tell your conscious mind that it is absolutely reasonable that it doesn't understand what the Archangel Raphael smelt like. And then ask yourself, "But if I did know, what would it be like?" In the next moment pretend you do know and let in a subtle awareness of what the perfume of the Archangel Raphael would be like.

In the same way we can understand the nature of our own consciousness. The following is a meditation that will allow you to do this. In this meditation the sphere of consciousness around you is referred to as your *feeling body*. When we connect to the *feeling body* that is around us, we are actually connecting to our own consciousness; the consciousness that we truly are beyond the physical realm. In this place, we can perceive multi-dimensional realities and connect to energies too fine to see.

Meditation to Connect to Your Sphere of Consciousness

The best way to get the full effect of this wonderful meditation is to read it into a voice recorder for yourself and then relax and listen to it. Doing a meditation to our own voice has a very special energy to

Christine Core

it, so do give it a go. Take it slowly, giving yourself plenty of time to pick up each quality. Just reading this will be an activation.

Close your eyes and sit in a poised but relaxed position. Take two deep breaths with the intention on the out-breath of letting go of everything that does not need to be in this space for this meditation.

Reconnect with the physical body by feeling the strongest sensation that it is giving you at the moment. Then allow the stillness of your physical body to quiet the mind. Breathe, relax, and feel its stillness.

Maintaining an awareness of the physical body extend your perception to the space in front of you. It is easy to project your consciousness into that space. It is actually part of you, part of your consciousness. As you sense or feel this space ask yourself, "If it had a colour, what colour would it be? If it was making a sound or had a song to sing, what would it sound like? If it had a texture, what texture would it be? If it was emitting a perfume, what would it smell like? If it had a flavour, what would it taste like?" Just allow the space in front of you to communicate its nature and qualities.

Now from the stillness of your physical body, take your awareness to the space behind you. What does that feel like? As you sense or feel this space ask yourself, "If it had a colour, what colour would it be? If it was making a sound or had a song to sing, what would it sound like? If it had a texture, what texture would it be? If it was emitting a perfume, what would it smell like? If it had a flavour, what would it taste like?" Just allow the space behind you to communicate its nature and qualities.

And now from the stillness of your physical body, take your awareness to the space on your right. There may be somebody in this space but your consciousness also holds that space. As you sense or feel this space ask yourself, "If it had a colour, what colour would it be? If it was making a sound or had a song to sing, what would it sound like? If it had a texture, what texture would it be? If it was emitting a perfume, what would it smell like? If it had a flavour, what would it taste like?" Just allow the space on your right to communicate its nature and qualities.

And now from the stillness of your physical body, take your awareness to the space on your left. Again there may be a person in this space and they will influence the energy of the space, but just feel your consciousness that is to the left of you. As you sense or feel this space ask yourself, "if it had a colour, what colour would it be? If it was making a sound or had a song to sing, what would it sound like? If it had a texture, what texture would it be? If it was emitting a perfume, what would it smell like? If it had a flavour, what would it taste like?" Just allow the space on the left of you to communicate its nature and qualities.

Now from that central stillness of your physical body extend your feeling awareness into all of these four directions simultaneously. You will now perceive yourself as a circle of consciousness.

Now bring your awareness back to the central still place of your physical body. Take your awareness to the space above your head. As you sense or feel this space ask yourself, "If it had a colour, what colour would it be? If it was making a sound or had a song to sing, what would it sound like? If it had a texture, what texture would it be? If it was emitting a perfume, what would it smell like? If it had a flavour, what would it taste like?" Just allow the space above your head to communicate its nature and qualities.

And now from the central stillness of your physical body, take your awareness to the space beneath you. This may feel quite different as also in this space is probably the floor. Allow all your awareness to merge with everything in this space. As you sense or feel this space, ask yourself, "If it had a colour, what colour would it be? If it was making a sound or had a song to sing, what would it sound like? If it had a texture, what texture would it be? If it was emitting a perfume, what would it smell like? If it had a flavour, what would it taste like?" Just allow the space below you to communicate its nature and qualities.

And now keeping your awareness on the central stillness of your physical body allow awareness to connect to your feeling body in all six directions.

This is you as a sphere of consciousness. Here are all dimensions and all levels of creation. Sit in the energy of the sphere for a while.

Now take your awareness to the edge of the sphere in front of you. Turn round and look at the physical body. How do you perceive the physical self? What do you think or feel about it?

In that space gently ask yourself the question, "Who Am I?" And sit in this space for a while. Repeat the question several times.

Now return the focus of your awareness to the still central place of the physical body and feel again yourself as the sphere of consciousness.

Hold the intention that from now on you will know yourself not just as a physical self but as this greater consciousness.

Because you have not disconnected from the physical reality it should be easy to now simply open your eyes.

This is a meditation worth repeating as it will integrate and connect the conscious mind with our consciousness on all dimensional levels. The dimensions are not separate and in layers like a cake they are a symphony of creation that is interwoven all around us. Angels exist on this multi-dimensional level. In fact, they only manifest on the sixth dimensional and above. Using this method of fine-tuning your connection with your own multi-dimensional consciousness will allow a deepening intimate relationship with the angelic kingdom.

A further way of developing this connection is to use our very accurate and well-developed sense of the qualities of colour as a way of connecting to angelic consciousness. As was shown earlier in this chapter, each Archangel has a colour associated with it and this colour represents the feeling, essence and qualities of that Archangel.

Angelic Reiki

The following meditation will not only allow you to perceive and feel the essence of ten archangels but it will also keep your connection with them. It is like an attunement and blessing from these archangels. By repeating this meditation, you, and everything in your life will take on an angelic quality. The Angels used in this meditation are the same as in the earlier part of this chapter. They are the ten archangels of creation that are to be found in the Tree of Life.

Meditation to Create a Deeper Connection to the Archangels through Colour

The best way to get the full effect of this wonderful meditation is to read it into a voice recorder for yourself and then relax and listen to it. Doing a meditation to our own voice has a very special energy to it, so do give it a go. Take it very slowly with lots of pauses giving yourself time to really feel the energy. Just reading this will be an activation.

First check you are sitting comfortably, poised and relaxed. Take two deep breaths with the intention on the out-breath of letting go of anything that does not need to be in this space at this time for this meditation. Bring your awareness to the physical body and focus on the sensations the physical body is giving you. Allow this focus and your gentle rhythmic breath to quiet and relax the mind. Take a few moments to do this.

Now take your awareness to the vibration and qualities of your consciousness, your feeling body that is around you in every direction. Take a few moments to perceive the qualities.

I now invoke the energy of Archangel Metatron. There is no colour just pure brilliance. Breathe in as if you were not breathing air but breathing pure brilliance. Hold the intention to simply become pure brilliance. How does it feel to be pure brilliance? Rest for a few moments in the qualities of Archangel Metatron.

I now invoke the energy of Archangel Ratziel and the colour is shimmering opalescent grey. Breathe in the colour of opalescent grey. What would it feel like if you had to become opalescent grey? Continue to breathe this

Christine Core

colour and become this vibration. How does it feel to be a pleasant grey? Rest for a few moments in the qualities of Archangel Ratziel.

Next I invoke the energy of Archangel Tzaphkiel. This is the highest vibration of the Divine Feminine and the colour is deep, boundless, sumptuous velvet black. Breathe in the vibration of this velvet black energy. Abandon yourself into its boundlessness. Let go and become the boundless Divine Feminine. What does it feel like to be deep, boundless, sumptuous velvet black? Rest for a few moments in the qualities of Archangel Tzaphkiel.

Next I invoke the energy of Archangel Tzadkiel. The colour is vibrant sparkling electric blue. Breathe in this blue Light. Become blue. What does it feel like to be blue? Rest for a few moments in the qualities of Archangel Tzadkiel.

Next I invoke the Archangel Khamael (Chamiel). The colour is scarlet red. Breathe, see, become scarlet red. What would it feel like if you were scarlet? Rest for a few moments in the qualities of Archangel Khamael.

I now invoke the energy of Archangel Raphael. Raphael's colour is vibrant shimmering yellow. Breathe in yellow. See and become yellow. What does it feel like to be yellow? Rest for a moment in the qualities of Archangel Raphael.

I now invoke the energy of Archangel Haniel. The colour of Archangel Haniel is emerald green. See, feel, become emerald green. What would it feel like if you were green? Rest for a moment in the qualities of Archangel Haniel.

I now invoke the energy of Archangel Michael. The Archangel Michael's traditional colour is orange; deep, rich, glowing orange. See, feel, become orange. Breathe in orange energy. What would it feel like if you were orange? Rest for a moment in the qualities of Archangel Michael.

Next I invoke the Archangel Gabriel. The colour of Archangel Gabriel is a sumptuous royal violet. Breathe, feel, see become violet. What would it feel like if you were violet? Rest for a moment in the qualities of Archangel Gabriel.

Angelic Reiki

I now invoke Archangel Sandalphon. The grounding colours of Archangel Sandalphon, the twin brother of Metatron, are citrine, olive, russet and black. Breathe in the colours of citrine, olive, russet and black. See, feel, become these grounding Earth colours of citrine, olive, russet and black. What does it feel like to become these colours? Rest for a moment in the qualities of Archangel Sandalphon.

Note that as you become the vibration of the colours of each of these Archangels you become the essence of their qualities. Through these colours you can become the *Divine Nature* of the Archangels of Creation, the Archangels of the Qabbalistic Tree of Life.

Take a few deep breaths. Connect your consciousness with your physical body. Recall the room that you are in and open your eyes when you're ready.

Chapter Six
DISEASE

We cannot understand the process of healing until we understand the process of disease. We cannot deal with something until we know what it is we are dealing with. As you will see in the following chapters an new understanding of disease totally redefines our perceptions and therefore the process of healing. It is the recognition of what disease actually is that allows us to move into a new paradigm and concept of healing.

The Truth?

Some of the ideas and concepts I offer in this chapter may challenge what you presently believe to be true. I am speaking from my truth, and as I will explain later, from the profound experience of being with Kevin during the years when he had throat cancer. If there is an idea I put forward that doesn't resonate with you, perhaps you could say to your mind, "I really understand that you do not agree with this, but just for a moment let's pretend it is true?" In accepting that the mind does not understand and telling it that it is okay and then asking the question "What would it mean if this is what is true?" can allow the mind to relax and a deeper understanding to reveal itself. Always honour your own truth though, but your truth beyond past conditioning.

Animals, plants and planets accept death and change in their physical bodies, but we don't. Hundreds of years ago death and disease were much more accepted as part of life, but today our modern medicine and the advertising and promotion that goes with it have created a belief that disease should be avoided, eradicated and cured at all costs. As I write this, I can feel how alien an idea it is to suggest that there is a flaw in the current endeavour to eradicate disease, but although it has been a declared aim for a many, many years, the evidence of any success is illusive. Could it be we need to rethink our whole relationship with pain, disease and death?

I would like to ask you to read the following list of beliefs and I wonder if any of them would ring true for you if you were ill. Some of the statements may bring deep, even subconscious, belief systems to the surface.

This is not a list of correct or false beliefs about disease. It is simply a list of beliefs that I have come across. You could also add some you know.

I inherited this disease from my parents or grandparents.
This disease has come from nowhere.
I am ill because of stress.
I don't deserve to be ill.
I am ill because I didn't look after myself properly.
It is an accident that I am unwell.
It is someone else's fault that I am ill.
My disease is punishment.
My disease is clearing.
I am ill because of my poor diet.
I am ill because I failed in some way.
I am ill because of the environment and pollution.
I am ill because of suppressed emotions.
My disease comes from trauma in my childhood.
God is punishing me.
I became ill because of the shock of a physical accident.
Children may think that their parent's illness is their fault in some way.
My body is trying to tell me something.
I catch diseases easily because my immune system is not very strong.
I am ill because of an infection virus that I picked up.
It is because of my age.
It is Divine retribution.
It is because it is my time to die.
I am unwell because of the weather or time of year.
It is because my Mother took drugs during the pregnancy.
I am unwell because of side effects of medication.
I don't know why I am ill.

Can you add to this list? How many of these statements do you believe are true? Do you know someone who believes in some of these? If you are a healer do your clients believe any of these? I recommend reading these a few times or even writing the list down. Your thoughts and reactions will reveal your opinion of disease.

You may be amazed at what deep beliefs percolate up from your subconscious and remember it is our hidden subconscious that drives and forms this reality.

As I said earlier I am not putting any of these forward as true or untrue. I have just made a list of possible beliefs.

Where Do My Views of Disease Come From?

It feels important that I should give some background as to where my views about disease come from as they are rather radical compared to mainstream opinion. First and foremost, they come from Djwhal Khul as channelled through Alice Bailey and recorded in her book *'Esoteric Healing'*. Second they come from my four years training and ten years practice as a professional homoeopath. The gift though that transmuted my intellectual information into a personal deep knowing was being with Kevin through the years he had throat and neck cancer.

Why Did Kevin Have Cancer?

Kevin and I were in a spiritual relationship for eight years and for all of that time his health was definitely not a 100 percent. In 2005 he developed an ulcer in his throat which became what the medical profession would turn *suspicious* and in the early summer of that year the suspicions were confirmed.

From 1987/8 (the time of the Harmonic Convergence, a time when many people's lives changed) when Kevin started meditating, his life had been totally dedicated to spirit. As I said in the introduction, this dedication led him to leave his job to focus on healing. Perhaps I need to explain what I mean by *totally dedicated*. Before he left his job in engineering he would get up at about 4.00 a.m. to do an hour's meditation and greet the day.

If it was summer, he would get up at dawn (in the UK the time that the sun rises varies from 4.00 a.m. in the summer to 8 a.m. in the winter). At work he would leave his colleagues at lunchtime to do a meditation in the storeroom, the only quiet place. He also developed the technique of meditating with his eyes open in front of his computer during office hours. On getting home at night, he would do an hour's meditation then go out to see his healing clients. He also found time to read extensively, but as I said in the introduction, not new-age books but those holding spiritual information that had been passed down through the ages. He was a natural intuitive healer and he observed many profound changes in his clients.

He was to channel that which the Archangel Metatron and Djwhal Khul used to bring through and write down this profound healing system known as Angelic Reiki.

In workshops participants would feel his energy filling the room. He was slight in stature but his presence was palpable. Djwhal Khul was an ever present energy around him. The room visibly changed when he invoked the Angelic Kingdom. He was sensitive, full of Unconditional Love and acceptance, generous, gentle and kind. Our Egyptian neighbours, who knew nothing about Kevin or his work, would comment that he was like an Angel.

Why had someone like Kevin got cancer?

It also seemed in spiritual terms that his life was just beginning. We were travelling and establishing Angelic Reiki in many countries and we were also teaching The Golden Heart Merkabah of Creation and New Shamballa workshops. Through his own research and personal guidance, he had a tremendous amount of information to share and wanted to write a number of books. He held the space in workshops that facilitated participants having amazing life changing experiences. He was also an artist and had not previously had time in his life to paint. We had brought with us to Luxor a box of oil paints and a full role of canvas. A rich life personally and in service was unfolding before him. We knew we had been together many times and this lifetime seemed to hold a particular poignancy and purpose.

So why would he get cancer?

As I'm sure you can imagine, this is a question we asked ourselves often and earnestly. I had spent ten years on my own and I really didn't feel I deserved to be on my own again.

Neck and throat cancer is generally regarded as one is the worst forms of cancer. In the later, stages it becomes extremely painful and can affect the Vegas nerve, causing nerve pain as well. Kevin was capable of extracting his consciousness from the physical body and thus reducing his experience of the pain, but even with an ability to do this the pain is so great that it is overwhelming; toward the end, only high doses of morphine made the pain endurable. It also compromises swallowing more and more as the disease progresses, which makes a dietary approach very difficult and in some cases impossible. It becomes impossible to actually swallow solid food, but liquids tend to travel up through the nose because of the blockage in the throat.

My purpose in sharing this with you is to demonstrate that what I am going to offer is my understanding of pain and disease comes from real experience and is not simply theory.

Spiritual Adages and Sayings

There are a number of spiritual sayings in common day usage that are profound and true.

As above so below.
As within so without.
What we resist persists.
Thoughts become things.
Creation is a balance of light and dark. Without the dark we could not perceive the Light.
Everything is part of the Divine plan.
God made everything and saw it was very good.
Nothing is good or bad but thinking makes it so.
Everything has a higher purpose.

At first glance, we all probably understand and agree with these truths, but when it comes to disease we find it very difficult to totally embrace any of these. We have thrown them out of the window and created a new list of beliefs. If we look back at the list of common beliefs about disease none of them fit with this list of truths.

Just consider for a moment the truth that *what we resist persists*. Disease must be the thing we endeavour to avoid more than anything else; in fact it seems strange to think otherwise.

As you reflect on this I would like to offer a channelling given to me by Djwhal Khul.

Channelling from Djwhal on Disease

By Christine.

I am Djwhal Khul.

> *"Dear beings who grace the Earth with your presence and your spiritual essence please know what you term disease is not a consequence of wrongdoing or wrong thought. In the place of Unconditional Love, in the place from which we see humanity, duality melts away. We observe that you have embraced such strong opinions of what is acceptable and what is not acceptable, what is right and what is wrong. From the great Love that we have for you we ask you to start to embrace a feeling of Unconditional Love for all things and all states of being. This is the essence of true healing. Disease in all its forms is not an ill to be fixed. Disease is not the result of wrong human thought or wrong doing it is purifying and literally part of the process of change."*

Disease is simply the symptoms of change.

> *"My dear friend, The Ascended Master Kuthumi often directs this channel to look at nature for a deeper understanding of anything that she is struggling to understand. The natural Kingdom around you holds great lessons. Consider the beauty of your trees. In the springtime they grow their leaves and buds form. These buds, in the*

fullness of the late spring and the early summer, blossom bringing the most beautiful scent and colours. Indeed the birds, insects and bees feast on their nectar. In late summer fruit is born feeding the animals and the birds. Then autumn comes, the fruit falls, the flowers have already gone, the leaves start to fall and the once beautiful tree stands naked unable to feed the life around it, bear fruit or express its beauty. Planets, they too grow and express their beauty and at some stage in eons are destroyed. This is the cycle of life. It is not good and it is not bad. It is the nature of existence in this universe and we too experience these cycles of change.

Perhaps you're asking, "What of the suffering of humanity, the pain which disease brings?" This is one of the gravest symptoms created by humanity's determination to fix things and not allow the flow of natural cycles. We have been deeply programmed into the need to fix disease and it is this resistance to the changes within the cycles that has created the pain. In acceptance, I can promise you that there is not the pain and the suffering you now experience. In Unconditional Love it falls away. In nature there is always a demonstration of truth and you can see all around you how resistance to change creates pain but in truth pain is an aggravation of energy that is not in flow.

You have actually used this principle of resistance to good effect on your planet. You use resistance to the flow of electricity to create the warmth which you need. I chuckle to myself now as you use all the Divine has created in a positive way, even resistance. With my great Love we now end this transmission."

I am Djwhal Khul.

The Gifts of Disease.

This is such an important message and in many ways a really difficult one to embrace. It is helpful to take a step back and look at all this indoctrination that has taken place and has determined our relationship to what we call disease. Indeed even the name has become to imply something that is wrong. So it is really helpful to take a step back and consider the process that has created where we are now in terms of our relationship with disease.

We tend to think of it as primitive to let disease take its course. In our arrogance we have thought we could eradicate suffering but there is still so much disease and suffering on the Earth. It is really hard to start to accept that disease has its place. A lot of the suffering we endure is because of our belief system about disease.

If we take a hypothetical example of someone who has cancer this is a possible list of what is causing them pain and suffering.

The physical disease and its symptoms.
A sense of failure.
A sense of letting down the family.
Feelings of regret.
Feelings of being a burden.
Feelings of helplessness.
Anxiety for the family.
Self-reproach.
Feelings of hopelessness.
Feelings of anger.
Feelings of guilt.
Feelings of anxiety about the future.
Fear of death.

This is the suffering that has been created by our attitude towards disease.

I would like to share with you a list of the gifts Kevin's cancer gave to both of us. I am not saying it was easy, it wasn't, but it was our process of constantly looking for the positive and the gift in everything that has given me an insight into disease which allowed me to start to understand Djwhal Khul's message.

> A time to simply be with one another without any expectations of the future just totally being in the 'now' moment and enjoy being together.

Gratitude on a level that I had never felt before. This gratitude arose naturally and passionately for the simplest of things. I was so grateful just to hold his hand or drink a cup of coffee with him. I was so grateful just to see the sun and the trees. I became grateful for everything. Gratitude brings one of the closest feelings of Divinity we can experience. There is a feeling of spontaneous joy, contentment and peace. It also brings a great sense of connectedness to everything. I wrote a gratitude journal every evening before going to bed. It is thirty-four pages long.

Our commitment, willingness and determination to embrace the truth that creation is always a balance of positive and negative energy brought untold blessings. We constantly looked for the positive in order to keep this balance.

As I said in the introduction Kevin was not cared for as a baby but now he had no choice but to be lovingly looked after. I know it was a great gift for him to know that there was somebody absolutely there, who would not leave him and who would look after him. We all deserve this experience some time in our lives.

We spent periods of silence just totally being in one another's company.

We enjoyed and appreciated the simplest things together.

We stopped rushing about and let go of the many things that used to demand all of our time.

Kevin went to deeper and deeper levels of healing the painful experiences his life had brought. Kevin understood his Soul's choice had been to attract in that lifetime an opportunity to bring all of his previous incarnations into balance giving him an opportunity to make this his last Earthly incarnation if you wish. It is not until we are made to bring everyday life to a standstill that we have the opportunity to do the deepest personal healing. The cancer had brought him this opportunity and I believe he took it.

Kevin had always been fiercely independent but now he relished the loving care of the district nurses and everyone around him.

He had not been close to his sister, but now they spent time together. During this time they shared stories about their child hood gaining insights and healing. Kevin died being closer to his sister than he had ever been before.

Ten months before Kevin was to die, we moved back to the UK so he could get the support and medical attention he needed. One morning, whilst we were still living in Egypt, I awoke at 4.00 a.m. This always seemed to be a time when worries surfaced in a very energetic way. I couldn't sleep so I got up. My mind rampaged through all the difficulties raking them up one by one. In 2007 movement for foreigners around Egypt was still restricted after a terrorist attack on a group of tourists at a temple just outside Luxor. Outside the city of Luxor we could only travel on the roads in armed convoy. The Egyptian government believed this was the best way to protect foreigners on their land. Tourism is the most important trade in Egypt and they wished to be seen as protecting foreigners, but for those who live there it meant that we were not free to travel. The medical facilities in Luxor are very limited and the nearest hospitals of international standard were in Cairo and Aswan. Both of these are around an hour's flight away. At four o'clock that morning I felt totally trapped and helpless. My mind listed all the problems: no help, no money, no freedom, no, no, no, no. And so it went on, creating a catalogue that described a totally impossible situation. It didn't matter whether all the information was true or not: it felt true and my mind believed it. This happened so energetically that my mind gave up. It reminds me of the phrase *"It blew my mind."* It did. It was too much and my mind literally gave up. In that moment there was bliss. As the mind released its impossible control of the situation, light flooded into the room and all that was left was stillness and serenity. The situation had given me what I recognised as a glimpse of enlightenment.

These are the extraordinary gifts of Kevin's cancer.

Christine Core

Djwhal Khul said in the channelling that what we term *disease* are symptoms of change. We can make it a positive experience and embrace positive changes. Once we do this, all of the negative emotional burdens melt away. In that moment when we choose to see disease as an opportunity it stops being everything that we have labelled it to be. Disease becomes a natural process of change and the gift, not a curse. I believe that we will not move forward in our understanding of the healing process and the removal of suffering until we are willing to change our attitude toward disease. I also believe that when we stop resisting and embrace whatever is here in Love, then pain and suffering stop.

Chapter Seven
HEALING

You could say that everybody is on a healing journey. If the planet is in the process of ascending then it must be affecting everyone. All of you reading this book will be on a conscious healing journey through specific sessions with a healing practitioner, workshops, or reading books and magazines. You are searching for knowledge and an understanding of yourself and the way forward.

So the process of healing takes many forms and, in a way, there are as many journeys as there are individuals on those journeys. We all find our own way. There is, though, one overriding perception that is common to all healing processes, no matter what it is, and this erroneous perception actually causes a great deal of pain and suffering.

I would like you to consider if any of the following perceptions are true for you.

Here, I am using the word *healing* to represent any process whether it is Reiki, all forms of spiritual healing, all healing modalities from Indian head massage and reflexology through to past life regression and hypnotherapy, and conventional medicine.

> Healing is a process of curing disease.
> Healing is a process of relieving emotional pain.
> Healing is a way of solving problems.
> I will be more spiritual when I have healed
> Healing is a process of personal improvement.
> I cannot heal myself.
> Healing will make my life better.

A healer has a training or skill that I have not got.
A healer will help me get rid of my problems.
Life will be better when I have received some healing.

I wonder if any of these statements reflect your understanding of healing.

For a long time, there has been the model of healing being like peeling layers off an onion. This idea can feel very true, but have you noticed how there always seems to be another layer? The belief system of peeling off layers actually perpetuates the process. If this is your model that healing is about peeling off layers, then this is what you will experience and it will be true for you. Peeling off a layer simply reveals the layer below and it becomes a never ending process. Have you noticed that the experience usually is something like this? The most important question is this, *"Has your healing journey brought you peace or has it simply revealed another issue?"* The journey typically goes like this. First there is a physical problem which does not seem to go away so someone consults an alternative practitioner. This problem is solved and an interest in a spiritual perspective on life is created. You go to a bookshop and pick up a book on spirituality. This talks about how our emotional problems stem from difficult experiences in the past, so we go to another alternative practitioner who can help with emotional issues. An interest in spirituality deepens and the next book that is picked up is about past lives. We can certainly see that some of our problems stem from experiences in other lifetimes. The next healing is past life regression.

At this point, we really feel to be on a healing journey and as the layers peel off there is an assumption that we are solving our problems and becoming more spiritual. But life continues to throw up painful things in difficult situations. We thought we were getting somewhere but new things are always presenting themselves and sometimes these seem to be getting even more painful and difficult. Perhaps, at this point, despairing hopelessness sets in as we thought we were making progress to somewhere and we had created an image of what this place would be like. We had expected that we would always be happy, life would run smoothly and we would be just expressing Love and Light. But this never happens. It may happen for a day or a week, but it is never permanent. We've set off on a journey expecting that there would be a destination and we never seem to get there. The Buddhists have a saying that the destination is the journey. It is only when we stop striving to improve that we can actually be in the *now* moment and appreciate and welcome life as it is.

We live in an illusion of duality. I am sure this is a statement you have heard before but it is important to consider what it actually means. The bottom line is that we judge. We are trained to judge, quantify and assess everything. Our very language is based on judgement. Probably, the first words you heard were that you were able to sit up before your brother or sister, or you slept better or worse than your siblings. From the first moment you were born value judgements were being placed on you. Our education system powerfully perpetuates comparison and value judgements. I'm sure you can reflect on your own schooling and remember how nearly the whole time you were being compared to the performance of someone else or the standards set by the education system. You were better or worse; you succeeded or failed. Value judgements are deeply ingrained in the human psyche. This is how the evolution of duality plays out.

The second way in which we perpetuate duality is due to how our brain works. The purpose of our conscious brain is survival. Its very nature is to reference information in the past and from that project the most likely outcome in the future. It is extremely good at doing this. This is how the left, male side of the brain functions. The trouble is we have totally taken notice of the left-brain and lost our connection to the right brain which intuitively knows the truth is in the now moment. In that place we are connected to the Divine and anything is possible. It does not depend on the past. It is due to our overreliance on the left-brain that works with duality and time that the idea of a healing path has become so dominant.

What if there wasn't a healing journey? What if, in this 'now' moment everything was perfect? What if there was nowhere to go and you were already there? From this perspective the present concept of healing has to fall away.

As healers we have been so locked into the concept of a process and something *to do*, cure, fix or improve we have lost the concept that in the *now* moment the Divine can be, and is found.

Christine Core

Healing is not a process of cure. It is an invitation to know who you are.

There are many books, workshops and videos on You Tube saying it is time to wake up to who you really are; it is time to embrace the greater self; you are god and goddess; you are Ascended Masters walking this planet. These phrases are all true, but have you noticed that when you read or hear these statements you feel good and positive but then, a week later, when you are back in normal life there is nothing happening around you that is different? You don't feel like an Ascended Master totally in charge of your reality.

The truth is that these statements can be said over, and over, again but if they are only heard on an intellectual level then they are simply interesting information. I'm sure you've experienced workshops where the experience was beautiful and uplifting but then the feeling had gone a week later. Or, you had a wonderful healing experience only to feel flat and depressed a few days later. What has happened? Why should this be? It is simply another experience of value judgement.

It may be surprising to realise that many, many people like being ill and most people would prefer to be in the drama of life rather than in the quiet stillness of spirit. This is not a fault on their part, it is simply a misunderstanding and they are looking for the Divine in the wrong place.

I would like to tell you one of Kevin's healing stories to illustrate this. A lady in her seventies had called him asking for healing and he went once a week to see her. She had arthritis. It was very difficult and painful to get about the house and she very rarely went out. Each week she was getting better. She was more mobile and the condition was less painful. Then, during one healing session she sat up and, quite angrily, told Kevin to stop. She said that she did not want any more healing and it was bad energy. We will never know whether it was on a conscious, or a subconscious, level but she was starting to realise that if she got better the district nurse would not call twice a week. The local social services would not deliver her daily meal and perhaps her daughter would not make time to take her out every Friday. What she was looking for was companionship, care and Love. This is what we are all looking for. Part of duality consciousness is we think these things come from the people around us.

There is a true, but difficult to embrace, spiritual saying:-

If it can be given, it can be taken away.

We are so locked into this myth of duality and separation that we are constantly looking outside ourselves to find the Love we are searching for. In this healing story this lady had decided she did not want to let go of where she thought Love was to be found.

Note:—As I write this, I am being shown that this lady had realised on some level that what she was looking for was to be found and always had been there, in the essence of Divine herself. She had retained this memory even though she had chosen to look outside herself for Love. This memory was present when she later left the incarnation, creating a greater ease in her passing into spirit.

Healing is the invitation to know we are part of the Divine, at some future time when we have improved or sorted something out. You are Divinely perfect now. Angelic Reiki is a *healing* process that totally envelops the recipient in the perfect and boundless Love of the Divine, The Angelic Kingdoms of Light. There is, in that moment, the invitation to know that, without any further processing or *healing*.

Have you ever asked yourself about what might be in the centre of the onion and why you can't go straight there? The still moment of now, seeing Divinity is in everything, is in the centre of the onion and yes you can go straight there.

You cannot go straight there though if you feel you need to improve before you are worthy of finding the Divine self. Nor can you go straight there if the healer perceives you as other than perfect.

Christine Core

The Healer's Role in the Healing Process

I feel the role of healer should not be taken on board lightly. Our desire to help others is often strong and especially if healing abilities are suddenly awakened because of an attunement. It feels exciting to be able to share this with others. This is natural, but it is also important not to take on the role of rescuer. It can be difficult to stand back and observe the situation, especially with a loved one, when we perceive that they are suffering in some way. It is a natural human instinct to want to help. It is not our job to jump in and sort out the problem. Everyone's Soul has chosen the most perfect life journey for that person. Sometimes from the outside this looks like a very difficult and painful process but there will be a catalyst for change and more spiritual awareness within that experience. I am sure you, like me, can remember difficult times, but looking back can also see the wonderful gifts the experience brought. It is important in our desire to help we do not lose sight of the potential beautiful gifts the Soul has chosen as part of a seemingly painful process. Unconditional Love is the healer, and unconditional Love requires that we can be with someone and embrace exactly where they are, without wanting to rescue them. This is to hold them with due respect for their Soul's chosen path. We have learnt through our difficult experiences and it is important that we hold a space for others to go through their learning process as well. Healing is a loving hand as we walk beside someone on their journey.

This is not easy, and this is why many traditions recommend that healers address their own healing first. In the Christian Bible it says in Matthew's gospel (International translation 2008) "First remove the beam from your own eye, and then you will see clearly enough to remove the speck from your brother's eye." And in Buddhism "Don't try and shine the light for another until you have found the candle within yourself."

Receiving an attunement is often perceived as a gift that is being given or something from outside that we are receiving. Sometimes it is seen as a qualification or achievement. Especially with the awarding of certificates, receiving Reiki attunements has drawn in many of the perceptions that are part of our Western educational process. A certificate awarded after an attunement is not a qualification nor is it a statement as to what has been given and received. It is never a qualification. It is an acknowledgement that the recipient is present. All attunements create a possibility, and only a possibility, for internal changes for the recipient. The Reiki symbols are archetypes or design patterns of consciousness and when we receive an attunement this Divine pattern is a catalyst that changes the recipient's consciousness. This only happens to the degree in which the recipient is willing to make changes and embrace this new energy. All attunement is our catalyst for internal changes and the possibility of opening up already existing potential.

An attunement awakens our own potential, which is in everyone, to be able to create a space of healing someone else. The extent to which a healer can do this depends upon the inner personal changes that they are willing to make.

In Angelic Reiki, someone who takes a professional practitioner's workshop has already been attuned to Angelic Reiki Master. To be attuned to Master is an invitation and gives the recipient the resources to understand and embrace self Mastery. I believe that this has always been the intention of a Master attunement and it has never been an automatic qualification to teach or heal.

Djwhal Khul is very clear in the book channelled by Alice Bailey '*Esoteric Healing*', that the consciousness of the healer is of the greatest importance. Angelic Reiki is both wonderfully simple and demandingly difficult. The simplicity is that the *healer* does not take any responsibility for the healing or outcome. This is beautifully taken care of by the Angelic Kingdom. The difficult part is the place of *doing nothing*, which requires of the healer letting go so that the Angelic energy can fill their consciousness, and the healer and Angel become one. This requires the healer to be Master of his own consciousness. The greatest support for this to occur is for the healer to have taken an attunement at the Master level. In Angelic Reiki the Master attunement is not a qualification to teach it is an invitation into self-Mastery and I believe this was always the intention in all forms of Reiki. Self-Mastery was a prime consideration for Dr. Usui.

It has always been the premise of Angelic Reiki to honour and embrace what is known as *The Ancient Wisdom*. This is to recognise the ancient truths that have, throughout the ages supported all spiritual practice. These are high demands and in the past have required a great deal of devotion. This is not the path of today, but this does not mean that we should abandon age old basic spiritual practices. It has always been an axiom "Healer Heal Thyself."

It is our duty to have a deep commitment to our own personal wisdom and healing first before starting to set up a practice as a professional healer.

The healer has a pivotal role to play in the healing process. What the healer believes and thinks does have a significant impact. It is exactly the same as the information that quantum physics has given us. The most significant discovery of those working in the area of quantum mechanics was that light behaved how the experimenter expected it to behave. If the experimenter's intention was to work with light as a particle, then light manifests as a particle. If the intention was to work with light as a wave then the projected light in the laboratory formed a wave. It is absolutely true that what we expect to happen happens and how we think things are is how they are. The intention and perceptions of the healer are of paramount significance.

This means that if the healer holds the thought or belief that the client has cancer, a bad back or emotional problems, then that perception of the person is held as an idea by the healer. If the findings of quantum physics are true then by holding this idea what the healer is creating in front of them this reality. On the other hand, if the healer sees beyond what is being presented on the surface and knows that this person is a spark of the Divine there are no barriers to this being realised by the client. How beautiful, therefore, is it and how important for the healer to know the truth of their own perfect Divine spark so that they can, unfettered by their own stuff, see the truth of this in others.

There is a beautiful story I would like to share with you. It was put on You Tube as an account of a near-death experience, but that is not the reason that I'm sharing it here. Don (just his name for this story) was hurt and disgusted by the way humanity treats mother Earth. The way we have used the forests, raped inside of her for oil and exploded nuclear devices appalled him. His view of humanity was that it was like a cancer on this beautiful planet. Perhaps his view of humanity was the cause, but I will leave this to your judgement, but he got cancer. He tells that when he died and was aware his spirit was leaving the body, he asked his spirit guides if they could pause for a moment and view humanity from the perspective of spirit. His guides agreed and they paused for a moment and looked back at humanity. He saw a mass at bright Divine sparks covering the Earth. In that moment he realised that whatever someone might do and whatever they might be experiencing, the truth was that deep beneath the external facade everyone was a spark of the Divine. He asked his guides if he may return to the Earth. He realised that he had been judging humanity because of its actions and missing the actual truth that the Earth is populated with Sparks of the Divine. His guides agreed to his request and his consciousness reconnected with his physical body. As his cancer healed and his new life unfolded, he had a new view of humanity and this view brought him great joy and hope.

As healers we can choose to either see the person as their problem or go deeper and know that they are in truth a spark of the Divine. The rub is that we can only truly see another through the eyes of unconditional Love to the extent to which we see ourselves in this way and deeply know that we are a spark of the Divine.

This absolutely does not mean the healer has to be perfect and conquered all their personal issues. It means that when we embrace ourselves in unconditional Love and all of our perceived faults and problems with total compassion, then we naturally embrace everyone else with Love and compassion.

In my early days of working as a healer with homoeopathy, one of my personal challenges was around criticism. As a child, my father's way of disciplining me was to criticise. There was always some fault with everything I did and I started to feel that I was no good at anything. I grew up easily interpreting comments by other people as criticism. This also manifests as feeling critical of others. I knew that this was not an appropriate state of mind from which to help others. My first task, if I was to be a healer, was to heal my own childhood pattern created by my father's constant criticism. Healing comes through forgiveness and when I understood that he was not meaning to put me down, but from his Love for me, wanted me to do the very best that I could, it was easy to forgive and embrace him in understanding and Love. Forgiveness and Love releases us from the power of any negative thoughts or programs.

Angelic Reiki Healing

The principle of an Angelic Reiki healing is that the whole process is the responsibility of the Angels, not the healer. The healer is there to prepare the place and to hold a space where the most perfect Angelic energy can manifest for that particular person. It is not the job of the healer to *call-in* or invoke any symbols, Ascended Masters or specific Angels. Exactly what needs to be there for the healing will manifest as a result of the dedication of the space. Any energy, whatever it might be, will be there if needed. If the energy of the Archangel Michael, for example, is required, it will manifest. So will any Master, Crystal energy or healing essence. As a human consciousness, the healer has a limited view. The most perfect energy may be a combination of Angels or an Ascended Master which the healer has not heard of. The most perfect healing may come from a galactic collective or a loving ET race. Psychic surgery may be appropriate, brought by a Master surgeon on the higher dimensions. We, as the healer, cannot know all this, but the Angels do. By holding an unconditional space totally dedicated to the Angelic Kingdom of Light, the most perfect healing energy will be there. It is in this unconditional, dedicated space where literally anything can happen. No two healings are ever the same because the Angels bring the most perfect energy for that person at that time. There is a beautiful saying: *'When we put out our own candle the Divine is present'*. This means that when we put aside our own judgements and opinions, indeed when we put to one side our personality self, the Divine can manifest in its purity. We are so used to having to take responsibility for what happens, it can be a challenge to totally abdicate all of our expectations, hopes and desires, and give the space totally over to the Angelic Kingdom.

I recall when I was doing healings for Kevin when he had cancer, that I had to be very aware of my own personal agendas. How could I do a healing and not have part of me hoping it would cure the cancer and he wouldn't die? But perhaps the cancer had a bigger purpose and part of that purpose was to end the incarnation? My personality did not want to embrace this, but perhaps it was the Divine intention of his Soul's journey. Simply being aware of our own personal agendas does make it possible for us to put them on one side. I found that when I dedicated the space and asked the most perfect Angelic energy to merge with me for the healing I could let go of my personal hopes and desires and allow the Angels to be in charge, bringing exactly what was perfect at that time.

An Angelic Reiki Healing Session

The first part of an Angelic Reiki healing session begins before the client arrives. The healer prepares themselves through meditation finding the still place within themselves. From here they can let go of anything that may be happening in their own personal lives and find the place of unconditional Love within themselves from which to receive their clients. The healing space is also prepared by dedicating it to the highest Angelic energies and using spiritual tools like candles and crystals to hold that energy. The clearing and dedication of the space is an important part of Angelic Reiki and I address this specifically later in this book.

The preparation of the space includes dedicating it to The Angelic Kingdoms of Light. This process fills the whole space with the vibration of the Angelic Kingdom before the client arrives. So when the client walks into the healing space they are literally walking into a bath of Angelic energy. The whole of the time the recipient is in that space everything is under the auspices of the Angelic Kingdom. All discordant energy is transmuted by the Angels into Love.

The first part of the session is an opportunity for the client to talk and express the reason that has brought them there. This fulfils a number of purposes but most of all it is an opportunity to talk. It is always a healing process to be able to talk about what is concerning us and to be heard unconditionally in a space of Love.

The tenet for the Angelic Reiki Healer is that we embrace our clients in Unconditional Love, without judgement, opinion, prejudice, projection, personal expectation or personal involvement.

Because the space has been dedicated, it is as if the Angelic Kingdom is listening to what the client is saying. This sets the intention for the healing and prepares the most perfect Angelic Vibration ready to step forward for the healing process.

This is not a time for the healer to collect information, but questions may be asked through them directed by the Angelic Kingdom. This will enable the recipient to find a deeper understanding of themselves. The whole process is about empowering the recipient to find their own truth and perceive, acknowledge and welcome that part of themselves that is already Divine. It is actually a great skill to be able to listen to somebody totally unconditionally. Usually when we are listening to somebody else's story, whatever it is, we are having our own internal conversation about what is being said. We tend to compare their experiences with our own and create a picture of what they are telling us based on our own experiences. In workshops I do a process which you might find fun to do with a friend. The group divides into pairs and I ask everyone to think of something that they would like to talk about. The job of the listener is to totally listen without nodding, smiling or making a comment. Whilst listening, they are asked to observe the internal process of their own mind. Most people notice that they create pictures of something that they think is similar or a similar experience. A process of comparison and opinion arises. This is what we naturally do in the process of everyday conversation and we are rarely, really, totally listening to what the other person is saying. We are trying very hard to understand what the person is telling us and we use our own database of references to do this. This is not unconditional listening. To listen totally unconditionally without interpretation and opinion is very difficult to do. The feedback after this process in a workshop tends to fall into two categories for both the listener and the storyteller. The storyteller either reports feeling embarrassed because they are not getting any feedback from their partner or they feel very blessed to be totally heard and embraced unconditionally, no matter what they had to say. The listener either finds it very difficult and embarrassing not to be responding to the story or they find a beautiful place of stillness where they realise that they are listening from the heart, not the head. It is not appropriate to be totally still and silent when listening to a client's story because they are not used to it and may find it strange or embarrassing, but sharing this listening experience with a friend will allow you to see how much you listen to them or your own story.

There is a healer in Israel who does nothing but listen. When he is listening, he is in a meditative state without anything going on in his own mind but he is totally present to the other person and with his eyes open. When our mind is still the Divine can be there. The healing here comes because the person is talking to the Divine and only unconditional Love is reflected back.

Second part of a healing session is the hands-on 'healing' process. The intention has already been set and the Angelic Presence is standing by to facilitate the most perfect healing for that person. There are no decisions needed by the *healer*, no symbols to invoke or call in and no hand positions to go through. They are simply there to hold the space that connects the recipient to their own most perfect healing Angel.

This connection is made by placing the left hand either on or just off the fully clothed body in the vicinity of the Higher Heart Centre. This is in the upper part of the chest, level with the thymus gland. Energetically it is our connection to the Unconditional Love of our Soul. The right hand is placed on or just off the abdomen in the area of the Solar Plexus. This is the connection to the incarnated being. It is up to the recipient whether the hands of the healer physically touch or not.

It is the most beautiful unconditional space where the Angelic Kingdom is those *in control*. They are totally in charge of the whole process. They will bring the most perfect energy. This may include a specific Angel, a Master, a Galactic healer or even a psychic surgeon if that is what is required. If a crystal or essence vibration is the most perfect energy, the Angelic Kingdom will bring it. There is absolutely nothing for the *healer* to do except hold the space and be the facilitator of the connection between the recipient and the Angelic Kingdom of Light.

The hands-on part of the session usually takes about twenty minutes and naturally comes to completion when the Angels signal the end. The healer will perceive a dropping off of the energy. If possible the healing is done to the music of Michael Hammer's CD **'Gift of the Archangels'**. Michael Hammer is a channel for the Archangel Yahoel (Yophiel) which is played on electric keyboard. If your parents were like mine, pop music of the '60s and '70s was the work of the Devil (at least), but it was the advent

Christine Core

of electrical guitars, amplifiers and sound systems that brought electricity and music together. This was an amazing gift, but I'm sure not realised at the time. Consciousness and Angels are both electrical by nature. One of the names for the Archangel Metatron is *The Divine Electron*. Music created electronically most closely vibrates with the energy of the Angelic realms.

Each recipient's experience will be different. No two healings are ever the same because they are brought by the Angelic Kingdom perfectly for that person, in that moment, and this can never be a repeated experience.

The third part of the session is to enable the recipient to talk about their experience, to share insights and ask any questions that they may have It is a time for reflection. There is a tradition of healers also being psychics. The healer's psychic ability has no correlation to their abilities as a healer. It is not the role of the Angelic Reiki healer to psychically pick up information for the client. This is important to accept both by the healer and the healee. Psychism is a valid and spiritual gift and those, especially in the Spiritualist Church, who can be a bridge between this realm and the astral plane provide a great service and comfort to those who wish to be in touch with their lost Loved ones. Psychism, though, is the ability to pick up information and messages from the astral plane. Angels do not exist on this level. Any information received by an Angelic Reiki healer will have been given to them by the Angel. More often than not, the healer's purpose is simply to hold the space and facilitate connection with the Angelic Kingdom. For the recipient to request information and insights from the healer is in fact giving away their power. One of the purposes of healing is for us to retake our power. Within us, we already know all of the answers and can find all of the insights that we need. The purpose of the last part of the healing session may be for the healer to encourage deeper personal insights and, thus, empowerment.

It is at this point that lifestyle issues may be discussed or advice shared. An Angelic Reiki healer never tells a client what they should do. This is disempowering and our whole purpose is to empower the recipient to know their own Divinity and, through that, their own wisdom and guidance.

It also may be appropriate in this part of the consultation for the healer to request information about medication the client is taking. It is never the job of the healer, unless they are medically qualified and being consulted as a medical practitioner, to give advice on medication, prognosis or diagnosis. It may be appropriate to recommend that the client consults a medical practitioner. Through healing, an interesting situation can arise where a client starts to require less of a prescribed medicine. Medically it is not often seen that a reduction in maintenance medicine is required. For example, if someone is on beta-blockers for high blood pressure, it may be important for them to consult their medical practitioner before a repeat prescription is issued. If the healing has reduced the blood pressure, which it may well do, then the maintenance dose may be inappropriate and even dangerous.

Sometimes seeking healing can be a way of avoiding the medical profession because the client is also wishing to avoid accepting what is actually happening in their body. Encouraging the client to see a medical practitioner in this situation is important.

At the end of the consultation, it is important for the healer to let the client go on a mental and emotional level. This is not to say that the healer should not make themselves available for support between healing sessions. In some situations it may be necessary for the healer to check that the client is okay. This is very different to thinking or worrying about a client after the session. If the healer thinks or talks about the client after the end of the session, the healer is holding the client in their consciousness as he or she was at the time of the consultation. That is the past. This can have an effect on the unfolding of the healing process.

On a recent workshop we had a discussion about keeping records of clients. It is obviously necessary in professional practice to keep certain records of one's clients. It is important though to be aware of what we write down because what we record is a statement as to how that client was. One of the participants of the workshop shared how she had felt the negative energy around the past records of her clients and had decided to keep her filing cabinet outside the healing space so that that space was clear of all past records.

Christine Core

Follow-Up Appointments

If someone comes for an Angelic Reiki healing with 'Ascension Symptoms', (please see the next chapter) only one appointment may be needed.

There usually is a correlation between how deep-seated a physical or emotional condition is and how many sessions will be needed. It also depends on how easily and willingly the client embraces change.

Usually in Angelic Reiki we see our clients once every two weeks, but it is up to the healer and client, with guided by the Angels, to decide when the next appointment will be.

I would like to tell here one of Kevin's healing stories which shows how a client can absolutely know when to come for healing.

One day after Kevin had finished seeing his list of clients at our healing centre in the North of England, as he left he found a lady, probably in her seventies, sitting on the doorstep. He invited her in for a cup of tea, (a cup of tea cures everything in Yorkshire!). She told him that she had just left the hospital where she had been diagnosed with cancer and given only a short time to live. She told him that she was terrified of dying. He explained he was a healer and asked if she would like to receive a healing. She said yes and at the end of the session asked if she could come back next week. The appointment was made. At the end of the next session, she asked if she could come every two weeks. This continued for about six months. It was not the cancer that was being healed, it was her fear of death. Remarkably, during this time, she reported that the cancer did not develop. This gave her time to come to terms and accept her death. Through the healing and the opportunity to talk about how she felt her fear of death gradually subsided. After one particular session, she told Kevin that she did not want to come back in the next two weeks but rather to book an appointment for the next month. During this time the cancer progressed but in the consultation she told Kevin that she was not afraid anymore. At the end of that consultation, she said that she didn't think she would bother booking another one.

Evaluating the healing

One of the things we humans tend to do is want to assess and quantify a healing session, or indeed anything. There is no way that we can assess or quantify the experience of a healing, and we do not need to. If the recipient experiences a great deal of energy, heat or whatever, this may be viewed as a *powerful healing*. If the recipient feels nothing, a natural reaction is to be disappointed or think that nothing has happened. But if we think of a river as representing a flow of energy, we only see or feel the power of the water when we resist it. When we go with the flow then we do not feel the power of the water. This is not to say that when we feel nothing it is a successful healing. It is simply to demonstrate that we do not know and that we have no way of evaluating the power or success of a healing session. If the Angels are in charge it has to have been Divinely perfect.

The beauty of this is that, as the whole process has been under the auspices of the Angelic Kingdom of Light, it has to be perfect. It has no choice. The Angels, beyond doubt, as an expression of Divine Love, know the most perfect energy to bring to anyone at any one time. It can be a challenge, but we need to let go of our human desire to quantify and assess the experience. The Angels can see the bigger picture.

An Angelic Reiki *healing* always follows the same principles as the spiritual work of manifestation. The intention is set, the connection to the Divine is made, and then we let go knowing that the universe will bring us the most perfect experience. The *healer* does not need to consider the success of the 'healing', its quality or if they did it right. All of these questions are totally irrelevant when we know that the Angels are in charge.

In the period between making the first appointment and the time of the appointment, the recipient may already start to go through the *healing* process.

The integration and process of a *healing* session usually takes about two weeks but the frequency and number of follow up appointments varies according to each individual case and is guided through the healer or recipient by the Angelic Kingdom of Light.

Christine Core

The Bigger Picture

There is a wonderful saying that the reason *now* is called the *present* is because it is a gift. As soon as we let go of striving, whatever may be driving us and rest in the *now* moment with gratitude, we find the gifts of this *now* moment. This is where peace, Love and bliss are found.

The following is part of an e-mail Kevin and I received as feedback from an Angelic Reiki workshop participant.

> "I am so thankful to Angelic Reiki. After I took my first workshop with one of your teachers, was the first time I experience Divine Love. My heart was placed in my solar plexus. There were no judgments at all. I was in that bliss stage for almost a week. (Oh boy, that feels good). What happened in that workshop was extraordinary for me. I came to terms and accepted my own darkness and my own light. Before, I would always try to get rid of my darkness. I discovered that I am a Divine being living in a human body. The density of the body itself is made of matter. The amount of light that I hold in my Soul will create the shadow, and from that shadow I will create my reality. And I also learnt from the Angels that day, that if I fight the dark I will give energy to it, but if I Love the dark it will lose its power. It is very tricky. Love does not mean giving in to it, just remembering that within the dark also there is light and those Souls that chose to hold the dark do so so that we can know the light. I still, sometimes get very confused about this, and just today I asked for clarification, and I know it will come; actually it just came right now, and I am again back to everything is right the way it is."

I do not think I can add to this. It so beautifully expresses that when Love and acceptance are in everything and expressed for everything, and judgement is no more, then the Divine is found. This is available to everyone now without curing anything, solving any problems or walking another step along the healing path.

This perception and way of being is not only applicable on a personal level. The same healing process can be applied to places, situations and events.

When we find this place of unconditional Love and acceptance within ourselves, this is what we also find in the external world. In fact, we cannot change the external world because it is a reflection of our inner state. There will not be peace in the world until there is peace within each of us. How can we look out there and hope to stop the conflict when there is conflict within our own inner being? In workshops Kevin would illustrate this in a really amusing way. He would ask the group if, when they got up that morning and gone to the bathroom, whether they had shaved or put lipstick on the image in the mirror! We shave and put lipstick on ourselves and watch the image in the mirror change. This is how we change the external world. We change the inner self.

Chapter Eight
The Ascension Process

I have already mentioned in this book the changes in energy which are occurring at the moment. These changes are affecting everybody. I've also mentioned that it is only because of these changes that we can connect to The Angelic Kingdom of Light in a new way. There is a lot of information, especially on the Internet, about what is happening at this time. Every indigenous peoples have in their prophecies that something special will happen around the year 2012. It is in the Bhagavad-Gita, the sacred book of the Vadas, and referred to in the Bible in the book of Revelations in the New Testament. There are also many differing stories and points of view as to what might happen in the coming years.

This process started in earnest with the Harmonic Convergence in 1987 and has gradually grown momentum over the past years. So far it has been a process, not a sudden event. There have been many signs and symptoms of this experienced by individuals, countries and the Earth. For humans there has been an increase in interest in spirituality and for the planet there has been an increase in volcanic activity and climate changes. I do not believe that anyone knows exactly what will happen, nor what the results will be.

There are some facts though, which are universal truths. Everything goes in cycles. One of the shorter cycles is breathing. Our in-breath and out-breath create a full cycle. There is the cycle of day and night which is created by the spin of the Earth, and of the seasons which is due to the Earth going round the sun. Our sun has a 26,000 year cycle around the central star of the Pleiades which is called Alcyone. The whole of our part of the galaxy has a greater cycle which takes about 26 million years and then there is a greater cycle which in the Bhagavad-Gita, is known as the in-breath and out-breath of Lord Brahma and this takes 8.64 billion years. All of these cycles come to completion in December 2012. This can be seen as an ending or as a new beginning. Much of the information put out is focusing on the idea that it is the end. It really does depend on whether you see your cup is half empty or half full.

The process that is taking place at the moment involves the whole of our galaxy. We are specifically experiencing it as what is known as a *quickening*. Scientists have shown that since 1987 the vibration of matter has increased (Schumann Cavity Resonance). The physical world is resonating more quickly. If everything is spinning more quickly then there is an increase to a higher vibration. This increase is occurring on every level, including for us. The idea of a higher vibration of energies being here is literally true.

For healers the most interesting part is how this is affecting the physical body, emotions, the mind and as on the spiritual level. I have had e-mails from people who are afraid that there will be a sudden change and humanity will divide into two groups: those who are spiritually aware, and those who are not. They expressed fears of being separated from their loved ones, family and friends. Moving into a higher vibration and therefore a higher consciousness means that we will feel more Love, more connectedness and have less of a sense of separation and individuality. If this is true, which it is, then the ascension process will mean that we become closer to our loved ones, feel more Love for everyone and feel more connected to everything. It is a process of uniting in Love not a process of separating from oneness.

The following is a channelling that was given to me by the group of Angels known as the Elohim in answer to a question that was e-mailed to me about the ascension process.

Channelling from the Elohim 9th June 2010

By Christine

The Ascension Process; What Will Happen?

This information, from the collective consciousness of the Elohim, came through in response to an e-mail I received expressing concern about what might happen over the coming years.

"The amount of information being put out about what might happen in 2012 and beyond is increasing. For some people it is creating a great sense of hope and for others dismay."

The dismay comes from the idea that two separate Earths are going to be created. One will be beautiful harmonious and peaceful, the other much the same as the world is now or worse. The idea of two separate Earths creates the perception that some people will not make it and that we may be separated from our loved ones who are not as spiritually aware as we are. I know of people who are asking the question "Would you go to a better place and leave all your friends and loved ones, or would you prefer to stay here?" The answer is often that they do not want to be separated from their loved ones.

How can this ever actually be the choice? Could the Divine creator, that is Love, ever come up with a scenario when one has to make a choice between living in a harmonious place or being with the ones we Love? The idea of this choice is totally erroneous. The idea of two separate realities being created is also not based on spiritual truths.

From one perspective, there already are two worlds. There is the world created by those who can only see the pain, and there is a world created by those who can see its beauty. It is all a matter outlook and perception. When you are in the company of loved ones and in the joy of being in that space, you are in the New World. When you watch the news and feel dismay at the chaos, destruction and pain, then this becomes your world.

The natural order of things is that there is destruction before the new beginning. The destruction is not less Divine than the new beginning. Planets, galaxies and the natural world around us all go through periods of destruction and rebirth. It is part of the human conditioning to regard the destruction as not as Divine as the new creation. In our personal lives we do not like it when things fall apart but feel great when something new happens. It is these judgements that cause us the pain; it is not inherent in the event.

The truth is that the world and creation is how we perceive it to be. What is going to happen over the coming years is the opportunity to see the beauty and not the pain. It is simply an opportunity and invitation. We can all accept this invitation whenever we wish. We can do it now, in 2012 or any time after. There will not be a division of either/or; a choice that will have to be made, and from the moment the choice was made, an irrevocable separation.

The idea that we can leave our loved ones behind is the same as the perception that death causes separation. We do not just exist on this plane, neither does anyone else. When someone die,s it is simply a transfer of awareness and on the non-physical level there has been no separation and never will be. This is the awareness which comes with the ascension process. Whatever happens over the coming years the worst that can happen as the planet ascends is that the truth of non-separation becomes more and more apparent and more and more real. It is impossible for you to leave anyone behind. It is possible for you to meet, see and embrace Loved ones on the level of unity and non-separation.

Where we are in consciousness, what we feel, and how we perceive the world, is the result of our inner state of being. Even those who are excited by the possibility of the new changes are looking outside of themselves for Love and beauty. This is just as much an illusion as the idea that the changes may bring separation and pain.

Ascension is the process of moving out of duality. It is a state of mind that lets go of value judgements, comparison and opinions. It is a state of mind that can see the Divine perfection in everything. Any notion that E.Ts, Ascended Masters or Angels have an agenda to rescue us comes from a perception that we need rescuing. This must mean that something is wrong and the Divine has made a mistake. Ascended being, by the very definition, see the Divine perfection in everything now. What is unfolding is simply a change in vibration which is an invitation for us to drop duality judgements. Dropping duality judgements brings Love, Unconditional Love, and that is something that we can choose to have at any time. It is simply that now we are embracing an understanding of this as a possibility.

> *It is impossible for us to see and understand what the experience of a new level of consciousness would be like. We do know its qualities though, and that is of more Love and Wisdom. This cannot be in pain or separation; however we may view it from where we are now. We are being requested to relax and trust.*
>
> *"The human mind is programmed to emphasise the negative. It has to be, because it exists to preserve us and look out for danger and difficulties. If we want to take responsibility for how we view the world, then this is the ability to respond, to look, seek out and recognise everything that makes us happy, that brings joy and Love. We can choose to do this or focus on the negative. What we focus on we get more of. This is the choice."*

The Symptoms of Ascension

An interesting and unique phenomenon has been occurring since the Harmonic Convergence in 1978. This phenomenon has affected virtually everybody on the planet to varying degrees over the last thirty-two years. It started, remarkably with what in the West was called *Yuppie Flu*.

It is important here to look at the relationship between the physical bodies and how we feel and how we think; in other words the link between consciousness and chemicals of our body. There is a lot of medical research that shows that what we think and feel affects how our nervous system works and the balance of hormones in our endocrine system. The endocrine system is our chemical communication and feedback system that influences almost every cell, organ and function of the body. We are familiar with the physical feelings associated with fear. It is not just an emotional experience. There is an increase in the amount we perspire; we get sweaty hands, and sometimes tremble. So just with the feeling of fear, the whole body changes how it works and this is due to a hormone that is released by the endocrine system. This is a relationship between thought, feeling and physical body with which we are all very familiar. It does not stop there though. All our feelings and emotions are preceded by a thought. That thought triggers a related emotion and a physical response.

Angelic Reiki

The acceleration of the Ascension process started in 1987. As this has progressed, we have become more and more aware of the changes that it is bringing. These changes have not just been the external ones that are on the daily news, but there have been great changes in how we think and feel. There are more people aware of spirituality now than probably since the time of Atlantis over 11,000 years ago. This awareness has increased rapidly over a comparatively very short period of time. The changes in energy are actually affecting everyone but for those spiritually aware this effect has been the greatest.

We have had a change in consciousness and a corresponding change on a physical level. These changes are probably greater than you would ever imagine, and have occurred quickly. It has sometimes been difficult for the physical body to adapt. This processor of adaptation has created physical sensations which have been very similar, if not identical, to symptoms of diseases.

The unique phenomenon, which many people are experiencing, is of physical symptoms being like those of the disease but without any pathology being present. At the moment, we have an unusual situation where physical symptoms are being felt, but there is no disease state.

This is a difficult situation for both healers and the medical profession alike. I have talked to many people who have either experienced for themselves or have known someone who has undergone medical investigation because of symptoms they were experiencing, but no problem was found. Not understanding what is going on here can be a challenging situation.

The Ascension process that the whole of humanity is experiencing is causing physical changes as well as changes in consciousness. In fact, it is impossible for there to be changes in consciousness without these being mirrored in the physical body. There are cellular, molecular and DNA changes. On a chemical level, this is involving the endocrine system and the chemical makeup of cells. Changes to brain structure and the nervous system are also occurring. There are also physical responses to emotional cleansing.

Christine Core

This situation needs to be handled very sensitively in terms of the information and recommendations that healing practitioners pass on to their clients. Part of our purpose as the healer is to pass on information so that the client can make an informed choice. Below are listed the *symptoms* which many people have reported in association with the Ascension process.

Kevin and I first experienced this phenomenon in our healing practices in the mid 1990s. We found that by making our clients aware of the various physical symptoms that can occur due to their changing consciousness alleviated their concerns. It is always important of course to recommend appropriate medical advice when symptoms of disease are displayed, but we found that for most people they intuitively knew what was true.

One of the main reasons Angelic Reiki was given at this time is to support us in moving gracefully through these changes.

Physical Symptoms of the Ascension Process

Headaches

These are one of the most common symptoms of change. Our brains are literally being rewired. As you probably know, generally we only use 5 percent of our mind's capacity and the good news is that more of its potential is being made available to us now. We also have used the two halves of our brain separately. The left-hand side is masculine, logical and analytical. This is the part of our brain that collects information from the past and uses that information to anticipate what might happen in the future. It is a very important part of our mind, but it is firmly fixed in 3-D in the way it is working at the moment. The right-hand side of the mind is feminine and intuitive. It already has the potential to understand that we are connected to everything. It does not see us as a separate individual. This means it can connect to a web of information, which is much vaster than the left, logical mind. It is from the right brain that we receive all our messages through intuition and insights, even sometimes predicting an event that may happen in the future. Part of the experience of being in separation has been for these two lobes of the brain to work independently and we have become over reliant on the logical part that only sees a limited picture. Therefore, as we move out of perceiving everything from this perspective of duality, the two halves of the brain are re-establishing connections. As our intuitive side becomes stronger and we start to take more notice of the insights and information that comes to us, this connection with the logical side becomes stronger and starts to influence it. Our brain actually responds in exactly the same way as training the body to any skill. If we want to play tennis or run a marathon, we practice the skills needed for this. The more that we practice taking notice of the intuitive messages from the female side of the brain the stronger these impulses will become and the greater the connection between the two halves of brains.

The knots in the Etheric aspect of the whole brain are untangling and this is bringing online some of the percentage of brain function that we have not been using for a long time. It is this that is enabling us to have new concepts and understandings of spirituality, creation and the world.

As these changes take place they are creating physical sensations and we feel these as headaches. Sometimes they are as strong as migraines and other the times they are simply a localised pain in a smaller area that passes quickly.

I recall when Kevin and I were teaching in Athens in the very early days of Angelic Reiki. We were teaching together as we always did and it was his turn to do one of the attunements. During this attunement, I felt an acute flash of pain from the left-hand side of my head through to the nape of my neck. It was nearly enough for me to call out "Ouch." My analytical left-brain questioned what this might be. It searched its database of information and came up with the fact that it was probably a stroke. In the meantime, the right-brain was telling me it wasn't and just part of the activation. This war of the two sides of my mind continued for a couple of days. When I let the left logical side of my mind take charge and fear came in, I wondered what I should do. Luckily when nothing had happened to me for a week the logical side of me starting to accept what the spiritual part of me knew: it was just part of the activation. If I had not had the information that pain like this was possible due to changes in consciousness, then I would have been most concerned.

Headaches can also be experienced due to hormonal changes and this is more common for women.

If you work in a spiritually balanced way, which most people do, the opening of the crown chakra rarely causes pain. It does cause heat on the crown of the head and this can be both just a sensation and a physical reality.

Another symptom we can experience is a general tingling around the scalp. This is due to the electrical changes that are taking place in brain function.

Loss of Memory

As these changes take place, our normal ability to remember things can change. I am sure a lot of you reading this will recognise this one. The main symptom has been, that, whilst long-term memory becomes more acute, short-term memory starts to fail. It can feel like a state of senility as you walk into the bathroom and cannot remember why you have gone there.

By far the best solution to this is to laugh. Worrying about all of these symptoms is part of the logical, left-brain function and simply tells that side of the mind that it still has an important part to play. All fear is generated by the left-hand brain which either references past information or responds to our fight and flight mechanism. Laughter causes our minds to relax. We can accept things as they are and not be concerned about this temporary state of senility. A new expanded awareness is coming online where are ability to remember the past and work out what to do is becoming less and less important. Synchronicity and intuition will take its place as we start to live more in harmony with the greater reality. It is a time of celebration, not concern.

Flu-Like Symptoms

This can feel exactly like flu and it is a matter of speculation just how much of the reported incidence of flu worldwide are actual the disease, or are physical symptoms of the Ascension process. The Ascension process is creating emotional cleansing. Every past event and emotion is registered in cellular memory. The American researcher Dr. Candace Pert has done a great deal of work on this. This of course includes all of our good memories and emotional traumas. Happy thoughts and emotions do have a different

Angelic Reiki

vibration than sad and traumatic ones. Specific research has been done on this; cataloguing the different levels at which various emotions vibrate. The lowest, densest vibration is that of shame. As our body and consciousness change these denser vibrations are literally spun out. The light that is infusing every cell and molecule of our body is dislodging all of these denser energies. On one level, we are experiencing this as a lot of emotional stuff coming up but it is also having a physical effect. This physical effect is experienced virtually identically to flu symptoms. It is very difficult to tell them apart and it would be reasonable to ask the question as to whether there actually is such a disease as flu. Every wave of a flu epidemic has come with a wave of energy that has flooded the planet. I leave this idea to your own intuition and discernment. As our body cleanses the lower density emotions, we experience a general malaise, lack of energy, changes in body temperature and sweating, dull headache, nausea, and lack of appetite and energy. These are also very similar symptoms to those experienced during a cleansing diet or fast. As our body cleanses, exactly the same process is taking place that occurs during fasting. Toxins, whether they are emotionally based or dietary and environmentally based, are stored in the deep tissues of the body. When we do something that triggers the body to cleanse, the first step is that they are released into the bloodstream. This is why we can feel so toxic when cleansing is taking place. This has been a very common experience and the best treatment is to, where possible, respond to the body's needs through rest and drinking plenty of water.

Changes in Energy

It would be wonderful if over the last few years we could all take time off work because our energy was low. It is ideal if we can rest when we are going through a period of low energy, but this is often not possible. Symptoms of Ascension can definitely cause great variations in energy. Sometimes our energy can be high, but generally people have experienced times of low energy and sometimes even extreme exhaustion.

I can remember when I was doing my professional homoeopathy training in the late '80s and early '90s. One day I was sitting at my desk in my little office studying the healing properties of the various remedies, and I absolutely could not continue. I didn't even make it out of the door but felt compelled to just lie down on the floor where I was. I didn't feel ill in any way I just had to lay down. There was no way I could continue sitting at my desk. It did pass in a short time and I soon felt okay again, but these periods of extreme exhaustion can be quite difficult to get through. It is really important not to worry about them and if possible take some rest. I guess I was lucky I was not in a supermarket at the time.

Great difficulty in waking up in the morning can also be a symptom. During sleep our consciousness is only tenuously connected to the physical body and sometimes the re-grounding on waking takes some time. Unfortunately coffee is not really the answer.

As our bodies change and new amounts of energy run through our etheric and chakra systems, we need time to adjust. Also it does require physical energy by the body to go through the adjustment process.

Chronic fatigue is rather a different situation. We are going through profound times of change. This can create difficult decisions and choices that we need to make in our everyday lives. Resisting making the changes our higher self and Soul journey have laid out before us takes a great deal of energy. This is one of the main challenges of this time. The left male, logical brain and the fight flight instinctive part of us resist change in order to keep us safe. It likes us to continue doing the same as we have always done. It understands and has references for this. To leap off into the unknown and take decisions which cause great changes in our lives takes courage. But if we resist these changes and allow the fear to hold us in a place of stasis, this sucks on our energy. The amount of energy it actually takes to not change is enormous. We are going against our life's path and pushing against all the changes in energy that are happening around us. This causes a state of ongoing fatigue. The problem then arises that the fatigue makes it more difficult for us to make the changes. So a vicious circle is created. At this point, people do need help to break free of the situation. Angelic Reiki connects us to ours soul-self so that its purpose can come through more strongly and we can find the courage and strength to make the changes needed. It is a time where we need to let go of control of our lives and follow our heart and intuition, and to the logical side of ourselves this may seem rash and unreasonable. The alternative is the tiredness and lethargy that comes with inertia.

Crying for No Reason and Feeling Emotionally Vulnerable

The new energy has caused a quickening in everything and this includes the molecular spin of our body which is literally spinning to the surface dense emotional energies like a spin dryer. We experience the result of this in a number of different ways. Sometimes emotions come to the surface. Spontaneous crying, feelings of anger or fear come from nowhere and there seems to be no reason. The answer is to allow these emotions to come up and not shut them down again. We can feel quite silly suddenly bursting out into tears for no reason but it is simply a beautiful cleansing. We need to be able to appropriately process anger without throwing it at other people or situations. Being still and simply allowing the anger to be there will cause it to burn itself out and the energy to dissipate. Fear is actually a normal and natural feeling of the human being. The animal part of our brain which holds the fight and flight reflex is a necessary part of our makeup. I cannot guarantee that it would work to send Love to a hungry lion bounding in your direction. The trouble is that fears entered our lives in many inappropriate ways. Not only does our memory create fear because of past experiences, but the nature of media and news reporting engenders and whip up fear and it is doing a very good job. Fear is a constant nagging energy that undermines our vitality and ability to think freely and make intuitive choices. Letting go of fear does not mean letting go of being appropriate, sensible and practical. Fear is by its very nature irrational. When fear is the driving force for decisions and actions it severely compromises our ability to make changes and choices in the best possible way. But as fear is part of our makeup, we have to learn how to respond to it appropriately, discerning when it is reasonable to be afraid and when it is better to put the fear to one side and make decisions from the heart.

Hot Flushes and Night and Day Sweats

These are quite common in both men and women. It has to do with the energy flowing too quickly through the body and hormonal changes. You may not be going through the menopause.

Muscular Aches and Joint Pain

Aches and pains in the muscles and joints can be experienced as a result of the changes. This can also be a symptom of cleansing. Our bodies hold toxins in deep tissue and part of the releasing process can cause stiffness and aching in joints. I have experienced a lot of stiffness and some degree of pain for quite a few years. After the death of Kevin, this became worse, sometimes actually making it quite difficult to walk. I went to a physiotherapist who successfully freed up some of the muscle tension. She suspected arthritis and degeneration of the hip joints. She gave me a letter to take to my medical practitioner suggesting X-rays and told me I will probably need to have hip replacement surgery in the coming years and it was better to deal with it now rather than later. I thanked her for the advice. I suspected there had to be a link between the increase in stiffness in my lower back, support issues, and right hip joint, male issues, and Kevin's death. It had got worse within weeks of his death so I felt I was holding emotional issues in this area of my body. For my own personal healing I use Angelic Reiki, Homoeopathy, "The Journey", created by Brandon Bays, and massage. So the first thing I did was book appointments with my homeopath and journey practitioner. I was in England at the time, teaching some workshops, so it was easy to make appointments with these two people. When I got back home to Luxor I went to see my friend, who deep massages every week. This was a painful experience both physically and emotionally. As she massaged the deep tissue, memories and grief surfaced. I went through a deep healing process for three months. I also did yoga and stretching exercises. Now I walk perfectly well and only have slight lower back stiffness.

Exercise at this time of change is very important and beneficial. Any exercise is better than none at all but taking part in something that also incorporates working with energy like yoga and *Chi Gung* is particularly helpful.

Heart Symptoms

Kevin published an article in 2004, which spoke of the link between changes in consciousness and physical symptoms. We received many e-mails and phone calls from people who were grateful for the information, especially for the information regarding the heart symptoms which are related to the process of change. Of course it is important for appropriate medical investigation to take place if someone is experiencing heart symptoms. It is also important to ask one's medical practitioner for information and clarification. The medical model is that if there are physical symptoms there must be something causing this and the most likely thing is some kind of pathology. This is a most reasonable and correct opinion for a medical practitioner. The consequence of this standpoint is that if there are physical symptoms and medical investigation does not uncover the problem then more invasive investigations are recommended. Kevin and I know of a woman in Greece who was experiencing heart symptoms and a doctor fixed a pacemaker even though no pathology was found.

Heart symptoms naturally cause concern and our fear of death can come up. This is not necessarily because we are a fearful person; it is part of our natural response to the symptoms.

There are two main ways symptoms of change are felt in the heart region.

Palpitations and arrhythmia are the symptoms that most frequently manifest and cause the most concern. For me the symptoms were mild and as I was doing a lot of athletics training at the time I thought that was the cause. Kevin's story was quite different. One day when they were particularly bad and had been there on and off for over a week, he decided to go to the hospital emergency unit. On arrival, the waiting room was full. It was early Saturday evening and all the sports injuries of the day had turned up for treatment. As he sat quietly waiting, the voice, which he now knew to be Djwhal Khul, suggested he go home. Kevin knew the energy of this Ascended Master well, he had been with him all his life and every time he had followed these messages he had subsequently found them to be right. So faithfully and trustingly he went home and commenced self-healing. Sometimes I could actually feel the bed moving when his heart was going through a particularly strong phase of arrhythmia. I would put one hand on his heart centre, call in Angelic-healing and gently his heart would settle.

As the energies of the Ascension change and we find ourselves more connected to the beauty around us and feeling more Love toward both those close to us and everyone we meet, the heart chakra changes. This change on an energetic and consciousness level has to have an impact on the physical heart itself. It has actually been shown that our heart beats to the rhythm of the Love we feel. It also beats according to our level of consciousness. We do connect from the heart. If our connection is with the world around us, our heart beats in sympathy and synchronicity with the physical world. If our awareness expands so that we see ourselves to be members of a greater consciousness, that of a solar system, then our heart starts to beat at the rhythm of solar consciousness. Many people doing spiritual work are now connecting to Galactic consciousness. We understand how the Mayan calendar uses a Galactic concept of time. There are writers channelling books from the Pleiades and other Galactic collective consciousnesses. When we start to perceive ourselves as part of a Galactic family, our hearts start to beat to the rhythm of the galaxy. It takes some time for the physical muscles to adjust to the new rhythm and we experience this process of adjustment as arrhythmia and palpitations.

The second category of symptoms is a dull pain in the heart area. This is probably being caused on an energetic level. The heart does not include a pain sensitive nervous system. All pain from heart pathology is transferred pain mainly being felt in the left arm. The pain I have personally experienced associated with the heart chakra is a dull ache in my back between the shoulder blades. It was more noticeable at times of grief.

Weight Gain

I don't know whether it is good or bad news to find out that the Ascension process can cause an increase in body weight! Our bodies are starting to recognise light as an energy and food source. This has caused changes in the way that our ATP molecule (Adenosine triphosphate) functions and also changes in the mitochondria of the cells. It takes the body time to adjust to the new intake of energy from light and it also takes time for us to adjust to realising we need to eat less.

Angelic Reiki

Another cause of weight gain is that with the increase in energy flowing through our energy and chakra system the first response of the body can be to increase its mass in order to hold this energy.

Mind and consciousness are electrical in nature, and water is a very good conductor of electricity. The changes we are experiencing can alter the fluid balance of our bodies. Diet and the use of herbs may be the best way to bring this back into balance. Stopping drinking water does not help and in fact it is often better to increase the intake of water so that the body's natural response to what it perceives as a drought situation is not triggered. The body holds onto water if it thinks it is not going to be given enough.

Feeling Spacey

Many people have experienced feeling spacey and ungrounded. Although this is a symptom of the Ascension process, I feel it is very important that we work with it and correct it. Part of our purpose in taking this incarnation is to ground the energy and we are not doing this when we are floating around on other plains. There is a large proportion of people doing spiritual work who are not grounded properly. This is usually not regarded very seriously. In fact a lot of people rather enjoy not being grounded. I feel it is an issue that needs to be taken very seriously.

The first point is very simple. If we are not grounded here, then we are not fulfilling part of our purpose of actually taking this incarnation. An important part of the purpose for all people who are working in a spiritual way, often called *Light Worker's*, is to bring higher energies into the physical world. Sometimes there is a great resistance to doing this and people will often say after meditations that they did not want to come back. This is based on a misconception that the more spiritual realms are somewhere in the higher dimensions. Just as light from different sources can coexist in the same place so do all of the dimensional levels, whatever level that might be. There is nowhere to come back from as all of spirit is all around us here and now. It is simply a matter of changing focus from one dimensional vibration to another. There is nothing spiritual about not being ungrounded. The concept of being grounded has been very misunderstood. It is a state of mind. It is the willingness to totally engage on every level with life on this Earth. It is to see the Divine beauty in nature around us and the Divine beauty in everyone. It is to relish being in a physical body and enjoying all the experiences and sensations being in physicality can give. It is a state of mind that has often been very discouraged by certain religious philosophies. New age spirituality has also perpetuated the idea that the higher dimensions and Galactic consciousness, for example, are more spiritual and more Divine than life here on this Earth. Divinity has no hierarchy or preferences. Everything is equally Divine and created by source/God. It is up to us whether we recognise the Divinity in everything or not.

Being ungrounded is actually quite unhealthy on every level, including the physical, and can contribute to the exacerbation of other Ascension symptoms especially fatigue. Our life force energy, Chi or Prana filters through our etheric body bringing energy to the physical body. If we are always 'off planet' then this life-giving energy does not flow fully through our etheric body in the way it should. Physical exercises and breathing practices like Pranayama strengthen our connection to Chi energy bringing vitality and health.

Pains in the Ears and Hearing Problems

Ringing in the ears is a common symptom and sometimes there may be pain. It can often seem like tinnitus and can be quite disconcerting. Many animals do not just hear through the ears. They are capable of picking up subtle energies. We can do the same and disturbance in hearing is the physical ear adapting to this ability. I remember once walking in the countryside, through the beautiful Yorkshire Dales, which were near my home in England. As I walked along the path next to the River Wharf, my ears suddenly started ringing. There was an increase in pressure and a slight sensation of pain. It only lasted two steps. I decided to turn round and walked back on that particular part of the path and at exactly the same point the same thing occurred. Looking at the countryside around me, it was obvious I had crossed a lay line. My ears had picked up the change in energy. We know from flying that our ears are very sensitive to changes in pressure and this ability to pick up subtle energies is developing for us.

Extreme Sensitivity

The changes are affecting our nervous system as well as the hormones in our endocrine system. We are becoming more sensitive. Some people are finding that their extra sensitivity means that it is difficult to tolerate some situations which in the past were normal. These can include loud noises, crowds, strong smells, certain types of music and even physical touch. These can be quite difficult to cope with but it will pass as we integrate ways of coping with our new levels of sensitivity.

Depression

This is quite a common symptom and especially prevalent in people who have experienced depression in the past. Depression is the emotional counterpart of physical fatigue. We feel depressed when for some reason emotions are not freely flowing through us. The word *e*-motion tells us exactly how it is meant to be. The healthy way to deal with emotions is to allow them to flow. As we become more spiritual, we will not necessarily encounter fewer emotions. There is nothing wrong with emotions. They are totally natural. Problems only arise when we do not allow the free flow of this energy. Western society teaches us to control our emotions and this usually ends up as suppression. Letting emotions freely flow through us does not mean that we can throw our feelings around. The free flow of the motion happens when we are still and allow the feeling to fully be there. As soon as we do not resist it, but fully feel it, it dissipates and melts away.

Depression can arise if the changes are causing cellular release of painful memories and we try to push them down again. The energy that it takes to do this is exhausting and leaves us drained and depressed.

A sense of despondency can also arise when we feel that we have done so much to release past pains and still stuff keeps coming up. In a way, it is a never ending path but it does end when we start to understand the positive gifts in what we previously thought of as negative experiences. This is the essence of forgiveness and it brings us straight to a place of Unconditional Love. This is the end of the searching.

Blowing Light-bulbs and Fizzing Electronics

Consciousness is like a web of electrical light. We know that we can detect brain function through picking up electrical pulses using the electroencephalogram (EEG), but *mind* or consciousness is not electrical only on a physical level. All levels of consciousness are like a web of electrical light. Part of the process is in creating these new levels of consciousness. This and the changes in our central nervous system can create an electrical field around us that affects electrical appliances. For some people this can be quite acute and for others it goes unnoticed. There was a time when Kevin and I dared not touch one another, and if we did we could actually hear a crack and see an arc of electricity passed between us. It was quite funny at the time, but as I am sure you can appreciate somewhat inconvenient. It is one thing not being able to get in a car without an electric shock passing through you but not being able to touch your Loved one is something else. Computers can be quite sensitive to this energy too. The phase will pass but also sitting quietly in meditation and asking for a rebalancing of your Lightbodys will help.

Dietary Changes

Many people are finding they need to eat less. This is a direct result of our increasing ability to transmute light into usable energy by the body. There has been a chemical change in many people that allows the cells to transmute light into energy. This is not only happening for people who are doing spiritual work. It has happened to the vast majority of humanity. This is a remarkable change. There are also changes in the type of food we want to eat. Many people doing spiritual work are being attracted to lighter forms of food and eating less meat. There is often an increased sensitivity to alcohol and other stimulants. Meat is especially dense and can affect the body's energy especially if the animal has been reared on hormones. There may be a strong desire for certain foods rather like that experienced during pregnancy. In a way, we are being reborn, so this is not surprising. This is normal and a part of the change to the higher vibration. It is important to really feel what you would like to eat and not go along with spiritual food fads. Not only do some people's bodies need animal protein, such as those with the C+ blood type, but sometimes the changes we are going through require an increase in protein intake. The main thing to remember is to tune in to what your body feels it needs. This is usually fresh, lighter foods like salads and vegetables. An increase in water intake does help the body go through all of the changes.

Animal Reactions

Dogs and cats and other animals will become aware of a change in energy and may be frightened or attracted by it.

A greater ability to connect to the natural world can unfold and we start to see messages from the birds and animals around us.

I usually sit on my balcony each morning and watch the abundance of birds in the trees around the villa. If I am away I like to take a short walk in the morning. During my recent trip to South Africa to teach Angelic Reiki, I went out one morning and my attention was drawn to a bird sat on a telephone wire. As I watched, it flicked its long tail and quickly turned around to face the other way. I just knew this was a message for me to look the other way. As I gazed in the direction indicated by the bird the sight was of the northern part of the Drakensberg Mountains. I knew this was important but I didn't know why. I asked the organiser of the workshop, who lived in that area, to tell me about these mountains. She told me that they had an age-old legend about a sleeping Dragon and they were quite a powerful energy vortex. As we tuned in to the energy that day we realised that the energy we were working with was causing this dragon Earth energy to reawaken.

During this time, we do need to take good physical care of ourselves. It is also important not to blame these changes or use them as excuses for not being able to do what we need to do. All of the physical symptoms we experience are because of our own change in consciousness. Yes, there is a bigger picture which involves not only the whole of humanity, the planet, solar system and our part of the galaxy. Nevertheless, what we are experiencing is due to our own personal response to these energies. It is therefore important that we take responsibility for what is happening and chosen a healing modality to supporter us in moving through these symptoms gracefully and quickly.

Christine Core

Angelic Reiki and Symptoms of Ascension

One of the main functions and purposes of Angelic Reiki is to deal with these symptoms of Ascension as gracefully and easily as possible.

In an Angelic Reiki self-healing, the left hand is placed on the higher heart centre and the right hand on the solar plexus. The higher heart centre is in the middle of the chest. It corresponds with the thymus gland. This is just behind the sternum about the length of the middle finger down from the throat. Spiritually this is the connection to our higher self or Soul self, the part of ourselves which is Unconditional Love and Divine wisdom. The solar plexus is our connection to the incarnated personality. One then asks for the most perfect Angelic energy for the healing to manifest. This Angel or Angels does not stand by the side but totally merges, infuses and penetrates every cell molecule and atom of the body and every level of consciousness. This intimate blending of energies allows the Divine perfect matrix of that Angel to bring everything into line with our new level of consciousness. This healing can literally change the DNA and cellular spin of our physical body, balance the hormones of the endocrine system and weaves the Etheric matrix of the body. This includes bringing the nervous and electrical aspects of the brain into balance with our consciousness. It will clear any *knots* in the esoteric aspect of the brain and allow greater percentage of its function to come online. As the male and female aspects of our consciousness become more into balance, a more active connection between the right and left lobes develops.

The gift of an Angelic Reiki healing is that the Angelic energy totally merges with us. This causes the patterning of Divine perfect, which is the Angel, to imprint this Divine perfection on every level of our being. We are like a symphony orchestra trying to play a great piece of music without the full score. Then we call on a great conductor who can bring all of the parts into harmony and create a single beautiful sound.

Chapter Nine
INDIGO CHILDREN AND ADOLESCENTS

There have always been special people being born on the Earth, but now there is an increase in the number of those with special gifts. They are mainly children, but this current wave of gifted and spiritually aware beings started around the end of the Second World War. The special children who have been born in the last thirty or so years have been given various names, such as Indigo, Rainbow and Crystal children. These names come from the energy around them. There is now an extraordinary number of these children and recent research and publications have documented their amazing talents. For example the Chinese government has recognised for twenty-five years there are what they are calling, "super psychic children". The abilities of these children are amazing. In research done with them, they were given a closed book and told a page number. Without opening the book, they were able to read accurately what was on that page. There are lots of children at the moment with phenomenal abilities, especially in the sphere of music and art. These children have talents way beyond their age. It is estimated that nearly 20 percent of children being born today have some special ability. Parents can sometimes find these children difficult as they have a great sense of independence and know their own mind. They do not respond to being spoken to like children very well. They are wise beyond their years and can see the pointlessness of many things parents think are important; such as school! Many Indigo and Crystal children are diagnosed as having Attention Deficit Disorder (ADD) because of their unwillingness to concentrate on what we think is important. They often have psychic abilities and look as if they are daydreaming and just gazing into space, but they are looking at what they can see on other planes of reality.

The time of pregnancy can be difficult for the mother of an Indigo or crystal child. In the chapter on "Ascension Symptoms", I described the connection between consciousness and the physical body. The mother's endocrine system and hormonal balance matches her consciousness. When an Indigo or crystal child is conceived, often a higher consciousness is trying to merge with the body of the mother. This can require a different hormonal balance to the one the mother currently has. The body of the mother tries to adjust to the new incoming consciousness. The hormonal rebalancing can cause a prolonged time of morning sickness. In fact this can last all day and up to six months. Not only is this very difficult for the mother but neither she nor the fetus may be receiving the nutrition they need. Doctors always try to avoid giving drugs during pregnancy, but sometimes if the mother is not getting enough nutrition, these are needed. Unfortunately the chemicals in the medication will not support the hormonal changes that are trying to take place.

Kevin and I discovered one of the gifts of Angelic Reiki very soon after the system was channelled. When a woman who had attended one of these first workshops became pregnant and was having a difficult time she phoned Kevin to ask for a healing. When he went to do the healing, after doing the preparation and talking with her, he asked for the most perfect Angelic presence to manifest for that healing. The Angel that came in for the healing was the one that was going to incarnate through this baby. The healing brought the exact balancing on a physical and consciousness level, the mother needed so that this new being could be born. Kevin found that this healing needed to be repeated about every two weeks for the first six months.

Angelic Reiki healings during pregnancy also created a link between the spiritual and physical worlds. This link makes the process of birth easier and also creates a greater feeling of home for the baby after it is born.

Older Children and Adolescents

We have also found Angelic Reiki healing to be very helpful for Indigo and Crystal children of all ages. When they or their parents are going through a difficult time, it brings harmony to the situation.

Angelic Reiki

Indigo and Crystal children integrate their abilities as they grow up. This can be an easy or a difficult process. This very much depends on the child. An Angelic Reiki healing helps them to connect and integrate with their talents and gifts.

Chapter Ten
CLEANSING AND DEDICATION OF THE SPACE

Angelic Reiki is a collection of spiritual truths woven together in a very specific way. It is the sequence and ingredients and the way they come together which creates this healing system.

An integral part of this is what we call '*dedicating the space*'. The dedication of a spiritual place has a long tradition. All places of worship are dedicated before they are used. The process of dedication is an ancient and fundamental spiritual practice.

This does not mean that this process can only be used for healing work. To dedicate oneself, or the day, to a particular purpose will support that purpose being fulfilled. I dedicate my office each morning to what I need to do that day. I might ask for the dedication to be for the day flowing well, guidance in answers to e-mails and the computer behaving itself. It really works. Just to say a quick prayer and dedication for anything that you do will make the job easier and the outcome better. It really does support all creative work whether this is cooking a meal, writing a letter or painting a picture. It can also be a very powerful practice in business, creating successful meetings, good decisions and harmonious relationships. There are Angels of money and business. (See chapter eleven)

Cleansing the Space

Before dedicating a space, it is important to clear it. The free flow of energy in a room will enhance whatever is done there. Physical cleaning and clearing clutter are a simple but significant part of the process. When the participants sit down at the start of the workshop I explain the process of dedicating a space. As part of this I asked them to place out of the room everything they do not need for that session keeping with them only the essentials. When they have removed bags, purses, coats etc from the workshop space and return everyone can feel the change in energy. Physical clutter is energetic clutter. The process of removing clutter from your office or home will always allow things to flow more freely.

The principles behind *Fung Sui* are based on the knowledge of how energy flows in a space. *Fung Sui* is a sophisticated science and in the East is used by commerce and banking. There have actually been court cases in Hong Kong brought by corporate banks that believed a new high building was interrupting the flow of energy or Chi into their offices.

There are many tools that can be used for clearing and moving the energy in the room; drumming, clapping, Tibetan symbols, water, joss sticks, incense, smudging, salt, fire (e.g. a candle), crystals, chanting, visualisation, dancing, music, etc. It is usually recommended to use a combination of about three of these. It is well known that when a vacuum is created something immediately fills it. So as soon as the room is cleared, it is important to fill it with the energy that you want. It is this part that is the dedicating of the space.

Clearing a space creates the free flow of energy in that space and only rarely is about removing negative energies. Removing negative and astral presences within a room can definitely be done with Angelic energy, but it is usually best to find somebody who is experienced in working in this way to clear it.

The Dedication of the Space

During the time I have been teaching workshops over the last fifteen years, I've come to realise more and more how profound this practice is. Even though we term this process dedicating the *'space'* it is important to know that there is no space. Everywhere around us is filled with consciousness and everything we think is solid is just energy. One of the great gifts of modern science is to show us that everything is energy. Even the concrete

I am looking at now, which forms the walls of my office in the villa here in Luxor, is simply a dense, compact mass of vibrating molecules.

The principles of dedicating a space are based on the spiritual wisdom of the power of intention. It is important to understand intention as the energy that *makes* something happen, not the energy of *hoping* something will happen. The universe is very literal in the way it responds to our thoughts and consciousness. If we dedicate a space hoping it will happen then the result will be a situation that reflects the hope that something will happen, not it actually happening. The universe and creation always respond to exactly what our intention is and it has to respond. It might seem incredible to think that universal energy has no choice but to respond to our intention. This is the extent to which we are Masters. In everyday life, we are not used to things being so absolute. The plumber may have promised to come the next day to fix a leaking pipe but then not turn up. The universe will absolutely not do this. Indeed the universe depends upon our intention and thoughts in order to know what to create for its next.

Around us, in our consciousness, is the symphony of all creation. The English language and all other modern languages are used and understood from the point of view of separation, judgment and duality. For example, the word *higher* is used a lot to describe energy and dimension and with it has come the ideas of higher up, more spiritual, better, desirable and so on. None of these ideas are actually true. If they were, it would mean that everyone at 37,000 feet in an aircraft had more spiritual understanding than those on the ground and that there is a very significant proportion of creation that is not Divine. There is no part of Divinity that is hierarchical. There is actually nothing that is more Divine than something else. We have placed a very strong judgment on levels of Divinity. I often illustrate this in workshops by asking the group how many would like to attend two new workshops I am creating. The first one would be a special way of connecting to the highest vibration of spirit. The second one would be about connecting to lower vibrations and the dense energy of matter. Without fail, they agree that more of them would like to come on the first workshop than on the second. Our very purpose is to find the Divine in everything and it is this judgment that has made many people feel disconnected from spirit here on Earth. This disconnection is totally untrue it is simply the non-recognition that the Divine does express itself in everything. The

Divine did not write any exclusion clauses like you might find in your insurance policy when creating the universe. Consciousness and creation are like music. The high notes are not better or more desirable than the low notes. It takes a myriad of sounds, high and low, to create a symphony. Consciousness around us is the same. We do not have to go anywhere to tune into Galactic consciousness. It is here around us now just like the light of the moon, planets and stars we see is here entering our eyes not many light years away.

We are the conducts of the symphony of creation which is around us. If we wish to bring in an Angelic vibration, then it is like a conductor bringing to the foreground the sound of the violins or brass. Part of this symphony of consciousness around us does not go anywhere. It is simply a matter of what we choose to tune in to. In workshops I never used the term "*I call in*" because it infers that that energy was in someplace else and separate. If we call for an Angel to come into a space, then where was that Angel before we summoned it? It was actually already here and an ever present potential for us to tune into. In workshops I use the word 'invoke' which more closely implies the truth that is simply about bringing forward something that is already there.

Knowing that we are in charge of the energy around us, and this energy is the infinite potential for any aspect of the Divine to be invoked, illustrates that we are the Masters and conductors of the consciousness that fills all space. Knowing this is the difference between making something happen and hoping something will happen. I mentioned in an earlier chapter that when we think of an elephant then that thought take shape and as far as spirit is concerned is a '*thing*' that is in our consciousness. A clairvoyant can see these thought forms. Cameras are also very good at picking up these thought forms and this is what is seen when orbs appear in a photograph. They are loving thought forms and if you have a good camera and can zoom into the picture you may see that these orbs contain geometric patterns. This is what a thought looks like. A few years ago Kevin and I did a Merkabah meditation in Luxor Temple. Part of this meditation is to fill the sacred shape or geometry of our consciousness with the pinkish purple light of unconditional Love. After completing the meditation, the group dispersed to look round the temple. One of the participants decided she would like to take home with her a photograph of where we had done the meditation. When she looked at the photograph there were the columns of the temple and in the space a large sphere of pinkish purple light.

Dedicating space is the conscious implementation of this knowledge. When we walk into a room, all of the thought forms and energies of the previous occupants are still there. In cleansing and dedicating the space, we can create the thought forms and energy we want to be in that space and most supports what we are going to do. Anyone can do this anywhere and for any reason.

Dr. Masaru Emoto has done some amazing research clearly demonstrating the power of our thoughts and intention. His beautiful pictures of water show that simply saying, "Thank you," to the water it changes and holds a pattern of gratitude. He also did a wonderful experiment with rice. He put two bowls of rice in his kitchen and every morning said, "I Love you," to one bowl of rice and, "I hate you," to the second bowl of rice. A few days later, the bowl of rice toward which he had expressed Love was still white where as the rice he had projected hate toward was starting to turn black.

Imagine preparing a special dinner party and dedicating the kitchen to that purpose and filling it with Angelic energy. Invoking in that space the Angel Anianuel will protect against accidents, the Angel Mumiah who brings everything to a happy conclusion, the Angel Ariel who will help you find new secret ingredients and the Angel Mihael who brings harmony to the family. It's much better than doing the job on your own! (See chapter twelve.)

For an Angelic Reiki healing or workshop the dedication of the space creates a bath of Angelic energy in the room. This is not just a beautiful place to be but it also has a very practical function. This Divinely perfect pattern of the Angels mingles and merges with everyone's consciousness. It embraces everyone with the Divine Love. It allows anyone to let go of dense emotions and instantly transmutes that energy into Love. It also means that the attunement into the vibration of the Angelic Kingdom is happening all the time not just when the healing or attunements are taking place. It also means everything the healer, teacher or participants say is guided by the Angels and that guidance leads to a deeper embracing of the Divine wisdom and truth.

We also have many spiritual tools which aid in dedicating a space and maintaining that energy.

Our Spiritual Tools

There are a number of things that will support holding the energy in the room. It is not necessary to use all of these but it is important to work with what excites you. It is the intention and Love with which things are placed either on an altar or around the room that is important.

Our spiritual tools for creating and holding the energy are candles, crystals, essence sprays, pictures, incense, cards, symbols, colour, music and flowers. Without realising what you're doing, you may be already using some of these spiritual tools. A room will always feels nicer with some flowers, nice pictures on the wall and a candle.

Because it is the intention that makes all the difference it is enhanced by doing the process consciously. The thoughts in our mind really do make a difference. Each spiritual tool needs to be chosen carefully. It is going to work much better for you if you feel a real loving connection to it and you see and appreciate its beauty. It is also important to prepare each item that is going to be used. Feeling gratitude for the gifts each item brings also enhances their effect on the energy in the room.

The power of the process is directly related to the focus and consciousness with which it is done.

Crystals

Crystals have been very popular with people doing spiritual work. There is a whole body of knowledge about their qualities and healing gifts. If crystals are of special interest to you, then it is l,ovely to create a collection, do a course on working with them or research information from the whole range of books that are available. This is not necessary in order to use them as part of the spiritual practice of dedicating a space. Simply finding the crystal you like, rinsing it in clear water, holding it in your hands, appreciating its beauty, and thanking it for its gifts, is enough for it to be able to serve you through holding the energy in a space. Quartz, like water has the ability to hold the energy of a thought projected to it. By giving it gratitude and Love it will untiringly radiate this back to you and the space around.

Candles

It is no coincidence that every church, temple and sacred place around the world will have candles. Candles are the highest and finest physical expression of spirit. To do any spiritual work and have a candle burning in that space invokes a deeper spiritual presence. The very essence of fire is transmutation and cleansing.

As I said in the introduction to this section, it is the awareness with which something is done that holds the power. A good example of this would be that if you are starting something new, don't relight an old candle. Getting a new candle specifically for the intended purpose, perhaps with the corresponding colour or perfume, will enhance the effect of burning the candle in that space. It is also recommended not to blow out a candle. Our breath is the link of our consciousness to the physical body. At birth the first thing we do is take a deep breath in and at the end of the incarnation we let the breath go. In using our breath to blow out a candle, we are using our connection to life here to extinguish light. I recommend a candle extinguisher is used and thanks are given as the flame is put out.

Pictures and Cards

There is a great choice of cards available now with pictures of Angels, Ascended Masters and symbols. The most important thing in choosing cards to support holding energy in the space is your connection with the picture. If it is a picture of the Archangel Metatron and you do not like it, it will not have a positive effect on the space.

It is also important to look at the quality of the picture. The science of radiologists has shown that the picture on a piece of paper creates a sphere of energy around it. The quality of this radiated field depends upon the accuracy and wisdom of the person who created that card.

In the process of choosing a tarot card, we are simply responding to the field of energy it has created and choose it by intuitively picking up on that energy or feeling it with our hand. The card's energy resonates with our own, therefore it is the one we are drawn to and this is why it reflects back to us our own truth. They never predict the future, just a possible outcome because of where we are at the time we chose the card. So by choosing a card through a feeling of Love it will radiate that energy into the space. It is also important to consider what message the card is giving. Pictures of Angels as attractive young guys with wings continue to reinforce in our consciousness that this is what an Angel is like. This is inhibiting our ability to connect with Angelic energy as the Divinely perfect creative power of Love that they truly are. Kevin and I have spent a great deal of time copying some Archangelic *Sigils* from an ancient manuscript known as *The Grimoire of Armadel*. This manuscript was discovered at the beginning of the 20th century in the Bibliotheque l'Arsenal in Paris and translated from the French and Latin by MacGregor Mathers. These Angelic sigils are patterns and designs that represent the essence of that Angel. Their root is mainly in ancient Hebrew but have a strong tradition in Western mysticism. Dr. John Dee the renowned astrologer, mathematician, philosopher and adviser to Queen Elizabeth I of England, used *sigils* to invoke Angelic energy. We have created cards using these sigils. We feel they invoke a purer Angelic energy than the pictures of human beings based on the paintings by Raphael and Michelangelo in fourteenth century Europe.

Choose the card that is right for you. It is important to find the picture uplifting and also be aware of the image it is projecting.

Christine Core

Sunday	Monday	Tuesday	Wednesday	Thursday	Friday	Saturday
Michaël	Gabriel	Camael	Raphaël	Sachiel	Anaël	Caffiel
Machen.	Shamain.	Machon.	Raquie.	Zebul.	Sagun.	

This is taken from the book The *Magus* by eighteenth centaury philosopher, chemist and metaphysician Francis Barrett. It shows the name of the Archangel along with their sigils, zodiac signs and *'heaven'* which it rules.

It is also important to choose your pictures of Ascended Master carefully making sure they project the right image for you. Find an image that portrays the spiritual essence of that Master rather than the personality.

Symbols

Many things can be used symbolically. On my altar here in Egypt I have statues of Horus, Isis, Sekmet, and an Anch. These all bringing the energy of the archetypes they represent.

Colour

Colour is very important in its ability to create an atmosphere in the room. There are many healing modalities that use colour and it is easy for us to feel the difference in a room because of the colour. The science of colour is used in offices and prisons as well as in home decor. By introducing the colours that you Love into a space, it can really change the energy. Colourful fabric is the easiest way to do this, especially as an altar cloth.

Incense and Essence Sprays

Incense is burnt in spiritual places around the world. One of the most evocative things is smell. It hardly needs saying as perfume is a multimillion-dollar industry and we all used it to either make ourselves feel good or to affect how other people react us. Aromatherapy is also known as a wonderful healing tool and its properties are based on very ancient knowledge. When using essence sprays, it is important to be aware of their quality and how they were made.

Music

Sound makes a difference to the energy in the space. D.r Masaru Emoto has also done research into the effect of music on water and found that the patterns within the water accurately reflect the qualities of each sound. We are very blessed today because there is a wide variety of spiritual music available and many of the composers and musicians have a wonderful spiritual awareness

Flowers and plants

I hardly need to say anything about the effect of flowers and green plants on the space. Providing plants for reception areas, office space and hotels is a billion-dollar industry worldwide. This is a measure of the impact of flowers and plants on the energy of a space. They make us feel comfortable, relaxed and welcome whereever they are. They also bring in the energy of the Devas and Elementals.

Magic

Magic has had very bad press for a long time and for a period of two hundred years, during the time of the Crusades, there was a concerted effort to stamp out its practice. Modern films also have done little to represent this subject in its true light and it is often associated with dark and mysterious ways and even evil. I mention this because I think it is time for us to remember the true meaning of magic and to use its powerful principles in our everyday life. The knowledge contained within the subject is about consciousness and our relationship to the natural world. Magic is to use the wisdom of how something affects an environment and from that knowledge create a particular outcome. You may have guessed that the whole of this chapter has been about magic. I encourage you to work with your own magical abilities and create around you in everyday life the energy and outcomes you want. This is part of becoming Masters and creators rather than living in consequence of events that just seemed to inexplicably happen around us. We do not need to live as victims of outside forces. This is abdicating our power. I believe it is time to reclaim all of our powers and use all of our wisdom and spiritual tools to create the environment in which we want to live. Many indigenous peoples have not lost touch with this wisdom and can invoke rain and grow crops in places where modern agriculture would not succeed. Many practices of indigenous peoples have been ridiculed, but I believe that they hold great wisdom and it is a wisdom we have lost and need to embrace once again.

Chapter Eleven
DEATH AND DYING

Kevin and I believed that teaching about the subject of death and dying was an important part of our work.

Kevin had done a lot of work with death and dying. He has supported members of his family through the process and he had worked for several years in a hospice in the north of England. All of the deaths in my family had occurred many years ago so I didn't have any personal knowledge of supporting someone until I shared the experience with Kevin.

One of the greatest services we can do is support someone during the dying process. We can also support ourselves by making preparations for our own death.

Death is the most important journey we will ever take but few people prepare themselves for it. Western cultures generally do not want to address the subject of death and this has led to it not being dealt with very well. In spite of there being many accounts of near-death experiences, we still feel it is an awful mystery and prefer to sweep the subject under the carpet. It is our attitude to death that is actually causing a lot of problems. Thanks to the hospice movement things have improved tremendously over the last few years, but still people are left in hospital beds to die alone. The language we use around death also exacerbates the situation. We talk about death as a '*loss*' and about those who cry as having '*broken down*'. The way we speak of death constantly reinforces an unhealthy relationship with it. We often don't know how to talk to somebody who has just experienced the death of someone close to them and avoid the subject, creating strained relationships. This can actually lead to losing close friends because they do not know how to deal with the situation. Many people do not know how to express their emotions and feel it is inappropriate to cry in company or in public. We also don't know how to deal with children around death and from the erroneous idea of protecting them, divorces them from a natural grieving process and contact with someone close who is dying. Kevin tells a story, which may also be true for you, of how when he was little the adults would huddle in groups and whisper about the member of the family who had just died and send him to his bedroom out of the way. This can leave the lasting impression on a child that death is something mysterious and needs to be feared.

It is a common event of all human activities, but it is the one we least know how to deal with. Death has been shrouded in mystery and fear and it is this that has created such a dysfunctional approach. We have also been fed misinformation and lies. We have been led to believe that nobody knows what happens, but this is not true. Indigenous peoples know what happens when we die, but modern society has dismissed their wisdom. The Tibetans hold this wisdom and today there is *The Tibetan Book of Living and Dying* by Sogyal Rinpoche, which describes how we pass through the veil of death. The Greek legends also have this information and are taught through the allegories of Hades, Persephone and Demeter and paying the boatman to cross the River Styx. There is *The Egyptian Book of the Dead*. This information was recorded by the royal scribe Ani and describes to twenty-one levels of the underworld, each with its own Pylon or entrance. It describes how we passed through the Duat and how our hearts are weighed against a feather by Anubis (the Jackal.)

In psychological terms, these texts give a complete description of the levels the unconscious mind has to be passed through in order to successfully raise our consciousness to a higher vibration. But even with this body of knowledge, we have chosen to buy into the idea that death is a mystery to be feared. Fear of death has so deeply been woven into our belief system you may be shocked to know that viewed from spirit death is a most wondrous initiation. From the point of view of spirit what we call birth is death. As our consciousness merges with the physical world we go through a band of energy that whips clean the memory of who we are on higher levels of consciousness. Very much like a strong magnetic field would wipe a computer hard drive. When we incarnate, we die to the knowledge of ourselves as being something more than flesh and blood and personality, but for spirit there could be no greater death. What we call death is the dropping of this limited view of ourselves and being re-born to the knowledge we are great beings of light. Yes, when a loved one dies it is very painful for us, but the fear and mystery around it have exacerbated the suffering both for the dying and others. If we knew that our loved one was going on an amazing journey and there would be wonderful loving beings meeting them and that they were returning to their family in spirit, then we would be able to feel sadness and joy.

Our attitudes toward death are changing and they will continue to change as part of the Ascension process. As we ourselves realise that there is just Love and no separation then death will lose its sting.

There is much for us to learn about how to embrace death both for others and ourselves. Death is the greatest initiation and journey we will ever go on but we rarely prepare for it. We usually prepare well for journeys, finding out something about where we are going, how long the journey will take, what clothes we need to take and who is going to be there to meet us. We can prepare ourselves for our own death. Kevin had done many meditations preparing himself for his own deathing process and this was not something he did when he knew death was close at hand. It is something to prepare for now. He knew which Ascended Master would come to guide him on the journey, what the journey would entail and at what level of consciousness he wished to find himself at the end of the journey. He was aware of the attachments that he had to the physical world and worked on releasing these.

The process of letting go of the physical body is a spiritual practice; it is an art. There is a good way to do it and there is a not so good way. At the moment most people in Western society go through the deathing process in the not so good way. This is actually affecting the spiritual consciousness of humanity.

What is meant by the not-so-good way to die? If someone approaches death and takes their last breathe in a state of emotional trauma, perhaps believing that it should not be happening or in a state of anger or fear, this conditions the place in consciousness where they will end up when they pass through the veil to the other side. The reality where they find themselves is totally conditioned by the frame of mind they are in when they take their last breath. How many people die alone with their bed pushed to one side and curtain pulled round them in the hospital? When we die, nothing changes. The only thing that is different is we do not have a physical body. After dropping the physical body, we started our journey. The next part of the journey is passing through what the Tibetans called the Bardo, in Greek mythology is the River Styx, in Egypt the Duat or underworld and in Psalm 23 of the Old Testament is referred to as "The valley of the shadow of death." All of these terms represent our own subconscious.

As we take the last breath, we enter a consciousness state where the whole of our life is revealed before us. So at the moment of death, we undergo a journey into our own subconscious mind where we are faced with rating the decisions that we have made in that lifetime and the consequences of those decisions. In Egyptian tradition, our heart is weighed against a feather. It is up to us whether we judge ourselves for what has taken place in that lifetime and it is also up to us how weighed down our hearts are as we let go of the pleasures and desires of the physical world. The whole process of passing through the underworld is an opportunity for us to release our attachment to the 3-D plane.

As we leave the third dimensional physical world, we enter the fourth dimensional astral plane. The astral plane is very similar to the physical world, Instead of it being composed of dense material, it is made of astral substance. This responds totally to thoughts and creates a reflection of our thoughts as the reality around us. If we enter the astral plane in fear and a great desire for material things, then all of these things form the world in which we find ourselves. In this place, time stands still.

Before I describe the next part of the journey, I want to let the reader know that the healing we can do for someone in the few days leading up to death is profound and I will tell Kevin's story about the death of his grandmother later. Because time in the astral plane stands still it is absolutely possible to do this healing now for someone who has died in our past. It doesn't matter how long ago. I wanted to give you this information here because you might know someone who would have greatly benefited but you did not have the information of how to heal through death at the time. Please do not feel regret; you can do the healing described at the end of this chapter, for them now.

Imagine someone who takes their last breath alone. They are feeling lonely and wish there was someone there to talk to; they have been regretting not being in touch with the son they haven't spoken to for a few years; they used to enjoy sharing a beer with their friends at the local bar; they recall how much fun they had had driving fast cars and wish to drive one more time.

All of these thoughts and desires create the reality around them on the astral plane, but it is all just a thought form. Here all the emotions, desires and wishes are felt but there is no way of satisfying them because all of the reality is simply astral substance. This is hell and we create our own hell from unfulfilled desires. There is no place of punishment except for the reproach we mete out on ourselves.

Just imagine how much we can so easily change someone's experience of death and the place in which they are going to find themselves after they have taken their last breath.

As there is no time on the astral plane it is impossible to say how long this state will last. Eventually the person may reincarnate with all their desires or these may grow less intense. There are people to help on the astral plane. There are many beings of devotion and Love and with healing skills. There is also a place where one can take the deep rest of astral sleep. If these desires and emotions are not strong and easily released, the person moves to the level of consciousness known as the fifth dimensional or plane of thought. Here the call of the Soul can be more easily heard. It is also easier to let go of attachments to the mind so transiting this dimensional is an easier process. The next level of consciousness is the Soul and with it comes the knowledge that we are not an individual inhabiting a specific location but a vast consciousness. With this awareness comes joy beyond what we can imagine, a passionate feeling of pure life and an overwhelming feeling of Love.

The Deathing Process

The process is in two parts. One is called the long death, and the other the short death.

The Long Death

The long death starts when a call is issued from a person's Soul to withdraw from the physical vehicle and return home. This immediately sets up an interior process and reaction whereby various chemical changes occur, and certain shifts in consciousness are activated to prepare the person for withdrawal. The timescale involved in this can be many years, a few months, or even a few weeks.

Some people are aware that the Soul has issued the call and for others they only know subconsciously. Kevin knew and it was when we were teaching in Texas in 2005. We had taught our first Shamballa workshop together which had taken the work to a new level bringing in the Angelic vibration as well as that of the Ascended Masters. We had now established three workshops together and Kevin received a distinct message that his job was now complete. We had to fly up to Los Angeles for the next workshop and then drive up the coast. I remember him lying on the bed in the hotel and really not knowing whether he was going to leave the incarnation. It was not the time for him to go then, it was just the change in energy due to his reaction to the call.

When the call is recognised on a subconscious level, then people can do amazing things to prepare for their death but not realise that this is what they're doing. A friend of mine's father started one morning to clear out his garage. All the jobs were completed (an unknown event) and all the tools neatly to put away. He then told his wife that he wanted to go on a long tour of the south of England and visit all his old friends. They had a wonderful summer and returned back home at the end of August. As autumn came, he became quite quiet and then one day he peacefully took his last breath.

It is said that even in the case of sudden accidents the person has received the call of their Soul even though it might only be hours beforehand.

On closer examination relatives can usually spot clues like finishing jobs, tidying up and making phone calls.

The Short Death.

The following was written by Kevin as part of an article on death and dying. The full script is available to down load from our website.

> *"'The short death'* involves a period of seven days. The first three days lead up to the day whereby the person will take his last breath on that day. On the fourth day, the person takes his last breath. For the remaining three days the person then withdraws from the physical/Etheric body and travels the path of return
>
> Why seven days? The reason is that seven is an archetype of creation. In the Bible, the world was created in seven days. In any one moment your consciousness is spanning seven days. In the now moment, where you are reading this article, is the fourth day. Your consciousness is projecting from this moment, three days into your possible future; and at the same time it is withdrawing from the three days of your past from this moment. So in any one moment your consciousness is spanning three days either side of the day you find yourself in now.
>
> To give an example of this! How many of you reading this article have found yourselves approaching a holiday and as you get closer to the date of your departure you find yourself finding it harder and harder to focus on your everyday reality. So if you were at work, as your last day approaches, you find it more and more difficult to concentrate on the job in hand, until on the last day before you go, concentration on work is virtually impossible. Why is this? The reason is that three days before your departure date a part of you had already set out on the trip. On the second day, more of you has left, until by the third day there is not a lot of you actually here.
>
> Of course this also works in the reverse. When you are on holiday, it can take you anything up to three days before you actually let

go of your life and work back at home before you start to really enjoy your holiday. As you begin to approach your leaving date to return home, you find yourself thinking more and more about what you will have to face when you get back. You start to latch-in to the problems you feel you will have to face when you return back to work or home. Again, this is because three days before your departure date you start to return home in consciousness. This is a cosmic archetype of consciousness.

Therefore, as you sit in the room reading this article your consciousness is actually spanning seven days and this is one of the keys to the understanding of manifestation, of bringing what you wish into your life in any one moment.

This is also the key to understanding the process of death, of withdrawing from the physical body. So a person who is dying goes through the process over seven days, takes seven days to die, to leave this incarnation on the third dimensional plane. There are three days that leads up to the day when they take their last breath. On the day before they take their last breath, whether that person has had a serious illness, or had an illness which has affected their consciousness, such as senility; on the day before they die they appear as normal as they ever were before they had the illness. I am talking here very generally.

They appear to be normal, without pain, in very good spirits, very animated and willing to chat in a very good humour. Everybody who is around them, their family and friends, are amazed and feel that a miracle has happened. However, this state may continue for about twelve hours, but soon after the person then lapses into a state of unconsciousness. Then, again very generally, that person will remain in that state for another twelve hours leading up to them taking their last breath.

It is here that I wish to emphasize that although the person has taken their last breath physically, they have not necessarily left the physical body. The process of abstraction from the physical body

Angelic Reiki

can take another three days. Their consciousness is still attached to the physical body for a further three days.

It is said that a person who has taken their last breath and is in the process of detaching from the physical body will be called back to that physical body at the same time they took their last breath, on each of the three successive days following the day they took their last breath.

In many of the spiritual traditions, including the Buddhist, a person who has died is not touched for three days after they have taken their last breath. This is to allow the person to complete the process of abstraction undisturbed. This is also why in the Bible, Jesus was interred for three days, and then arose again.

As in the example given above whereby we accept that our consciousness is constantly scanning a period of seven days, we can see how a person who is about to die has visions of people in the room that nobody else can see. This is because their consciousness is already transiting into the fourth dimension, so in actual fact the person who is dying perceives two realities at the same time. It is a truth, that as the time of death approaches, death being the last breath, the person that they were connected to most in a loving way, who has already passed over into the 4th Dimension, is allowed to guide the dying person through the process. For a person doing spiritual work, or an Initiate, the Master in whose ashram they are a part will come to guide his student back into the ashram.

Staff and nurses who work in hospices know the signs very well and can indicate to relatives very accurately when that person will take their last breath.

For me, the Irish have the most perfect way of dealing with death. When the person has died they are gently placed in a coffin, which is then placed in the living room of their home, and a three-day celebration ensues. As that person is drawn back to the physical body at the time of their death over the next three days they find themselves surrounded by all their friends and relatives in celebration of who they were. What better way of leaving the third dimensional plane than that!

The subject I would like to touch on now will certainly present itself to many of you reading this article in your lifetime. When a person is dying the senses start to become very acute, and this is very well known. The order in which the senses activate at birth now start to deactivate in reverse order at death. A person who is close to death will start to decline eating food, followed closely by declining to drink. The timescale of this is very variable. The last sense which remains right up until the moment of the last breath is hearing. This sense can become so acute that you could be ten feet away from the person and they could hear what you are saying in a whisper.

Our perception of being around the dying person is quite the reverse. To see a person close to death, you would think that they would be totally unconscious, without any attachment to physical plane reality whatsoever. Relatives who visit a person in such a state tend to voice their opinions of that person believing that they cannot hear them. They can quite easily fall into discussions about negative situations in which they found themselves and the person who is dying. Contrary to their belief, that person can hear every word and react in consciousness to it. This again can cause untold misery and anxiety to the person who is dying and an awareness of this should be made available in all situations where relatives are visiting a dying relative or friend.

The reaction of the dying person to what is said about them can create a situation in consciousness that will influence where they end up in consciousness as they pass into the fourth dimension. We must constantly be aware that when we are with a dying person all that we think, say, or do, has the potential to influence the environment in which that person finds themselves when they leave this incarnation.

It is here that I would like to deal now with the actual process of abstraction from the physical body.

From that part of ourselves which projects consciousness into the 3-D realm, a call is issued for that part to return to the whole. This causes certain reactions to occur which are as follows; a) This causes certain physiological effects to be felt, in connection with the heart, the nervous system, and the endocrine system. These effects are known to the medical profession and have been catalogued by them. b) Our nervous system has its Etheric counterpart and in the Hindu system these are known as the nadis. They are the electromagnetic energy filaments which penetrate every nerve in our bodies. It is through the Etheric body and the nadis that our Soul connects to this incarnation. They react to the directing impulse of return issued by the Soul and reorganize themselves for abstraction from the dense physical sheath. This is felt as a vibration which runs through the entire nervous system. c) The effect of the vibration which thrills through the Etheric nervous system causes a change in blood chemistry. This change comes through the glandular system which injects into the bloodstream a chemical which affects the heart. The life thread is anchored in the heart and this chemical starts the process whereby this life thread is separated. It also evokes a reflex action in the brain which causes loss of consciousness and/ or coma. d) Another vibration ensues, whereby the nadis, the electromagnetic filaments penetrating every nerve in our bodies, are separated from the physical aspects of those nerves. The Etheric body is thereby detached from the dense physical body but still interpenetrating it.

There is a pause at this time. This allows the above process to continue in the right timing for the person involved, with the least amount of effort, trauma, and as painlessly as possible. The detachment of the nadis is first evidenced in the eyes. When you are around a person who is dying, you will notice that close to the day they take their last breath their eyes change. There is a kind of peace that descends on the person, the resistance to dying goes, and they begin to accept what is happening. This is the time, no matter what the illness, where the person seems to be fully here.

It is at this point in the future when all the relatives and friends of that person will be in celebration around them; to celebrate their life together and to wish Godspeed to that person on their journey.

Next, the organized Etheric body, already loosened from the dense physical sheath by the nadis, gathers itself for the final departure. It withdraws from the extremities towards the doorway by which it will exit the physical body. These exits are labelled above. In a person who is dying, as seen from the 3-D plane, all heat from the limbs starts to retreat into the main trunk of the body.

At this point another pull is felt. As the vital body which has animated all of the cells of that body is withdrawn, the being which is the elemental aspect of the Earth calls back unto itself the matter of the physical body. Again, if you are around a person who is dying, this is evidenced by a notable pallor of the skin, which takes on a pale configuration and waxy appearance. At this point the vital body is preparing for exit, and the physical body is preparing for dissolution.

It is here that another pause can occur. It is also here where sometimes the physical elemental of the body in question can resist the process, and tries to retain hold of the disappearing life force which animated it. However, when death is inevitable and is overlighted by the call of the Soul, this pause lasts only for a few moments.

The Etheric body now detaches itself in gradual stages through the chosen exit until its emergence is complete. It is at this point, as we observe the dying person; they take their last physical breath in the 3-D world. Contrary to popular belief, the vital body which has now been released from the physical sheath does not travel to its next port of call. It is still influenced by the physical body, and this influence can persist for a period of up to three days or longer. As has been mentioned above, the vital body, which is the sum total of the person who has died, minus the physical sheath, is still influenced by that physical body. This can most definitely occur if the person who has died has had a very Earthly existence and has been attached to the physical form and physical desires.

Next comes the dissolving of the Etheric body itself. As the pull of the Soul continues, it causes the energies of which the Etheric body is composed to reorganize and withdraw, leaving only the electromagnetic/pranic substance of which the Etheric body was composed to return to the general reservoir of planetary pranic substance.

It is worth noting here that the process of cremation is recommended as a way of severing completely all ties to the physical body. Destroying the physical body by fire is a purification process which severs all connection to the physical body by destroying the Etheric body. For those members of humanity who conduct a lifetime centred on the dense physical, enjoying material pleasures, and coveting material desires; where the pull of the Soul is weak and material attachment is strong, this connection to the physical body can be overwhelming. If the physical body is not destroyed by fire, the attachment of these beings to the physical body can last for many, many years.

Conversely, the person who has done spiritual work and recognized the illusory nature of attachment to the material plane, will make the above transition very rapidly indeed. In either case, when the person has severed all ties to the physical body, they stand in their subtle bodies ready for what Djwhal Khul, through Alice Bailey, calls "The Art of Elimination."

As has been indicated above, there are three types of human beings in incarnation at the moment. The first is the person who is centred in emotional drama and the astral plane. The second is that person who is heart centred, whose focus is on recognizing that their actions affect others and take responsibility for those actions. The third is the person who has undertaken a spiritual path, who recognizes in consciousness that they are part of a greater life; they are connected to all things as part of that greater life and assume responsibility for that life.

Christine Core

The next part of the process affects each of these three groups differently.

This process is the relinquishing of the astral and mental bodies, so that the recently released incarnated being can once again bathe in the glorious light of their Soul.

In the person whose mind is undeveloped and has been centred in emotional drama, the elimination of the astral body can take a long time. It is done by a process of attrition, by re-living over and over again in the dense matter of the astral plane, all of those attachments to feelings and desires created in the recently requited incarnation, until such time as the person in question tires and recognizes the unfulfilment of such desires without connection to a physical body. Most of these desires are created through the animal aspect of the physical body, and without that physical body to feel the desires and experience them all is of no import. It is this recognition which causes the being on the astral plane to finally let go of these desires.

In the person who is heart centred and has developed mentally, the process takes two forms. This person feels their attachment to the mental plane and gravitates to it, letting go in the process of any attachment to emotional desire. Once in the mental body the person becomes aware, at that level, of the glorious light of their Soul, however dimly it may shine. This awareness of the Soul causes this being to reach out for it, and in doing so shatters the constructed mental body.

In the person who is spiritually orientated, in total consciousness, they focus on two things.

This person clears any attachment to astral matter or thought forms by calling in light from their Soul. It is this light which dissolves any attachment that this being has to the astral plane. Next, this being is given Words of Power by the Master in whose Ashram he is a member. By sounding these Words of Power on the mental plane, it creates a down—pouring of Soul power which causes such an expansion of consciousness that it brings about the shattering of the mental body. That being can now stand free in the Ashram of their Master and bathe in the light of their Soul

At this point, depending on which of the three groups the person is centred in, activities ensue that creates the future path for that person. Again, the mechanics of this is known but is not part of this article.

Some words here about the space that you find yourself in when all connections to the physical body have dropped away. Space and time as we know it no longer exists. A timelessness ensues which brings a clarity unknown to us in this physical incarnation. For those beings polarized in the emotional body they turn their attention totally on that body to work out unfulfilled desires.

For the person who has been heart centred, as the sense of time drops away they see the past, the present, and the future presented in one moment. Both for the being polarized in the emotional body, and being who has been heart centred, and is polarized in the mental body, as the timelessness is recognized, in that moment there is a Soul contact. The whole of the incarnation that being has created is revealed. The three major conditioning factors in that incarnation are presented, and all else drops away and fades out of their memory. It is these three major conditioning factors that dictate the next incarnation that being will take.

In all traditions there is a description of a place we end up when we die. Some call it heaven, various indigenous peoples have other names for it, the Theosophists call it Devachan. In all cases it is a description of a place we go to enjoy the fruits of good deeds. This is a misinterpretation. As the person going through the experience makes that Soul contact, and timelessness is revealed, the eternal Now Moment is presented in all its glory. As we travel through incarnation after incarnation, we come to recognize that all exists in a single point of infinite glory, beauty, and existence. For the person who has developed heart centeredness and the initiate, the full import of this now moment, is revealed causing an upwelling of ecstatic bliss. As this moment exists out of time as we know it, contacted from the 3-D realm, it appears to be infinite, eternal, without end. This is the heaven that is talked about.

For the spiritual person, the path that leads to death is a familiar one. They have spent a lifetime connecting to the higher planes, recognizing themselves more as Spirit than as the incarnated human being. They have spent many hours in meditation, raising their consciousness to connect with the Divine. They embrace the fact that we have many incarnations in the 3-D realm, and they recall into consciousness the many times that they have died before. Death has no fear for this person, because they know that death is life, and life is death. The death is not an ending but a return home where the glory of their Soul waits with open arms to welcome them back.

They know that the call to return has come for two reasons, either the physical body is no longer capable of holding their consciousness and in some way has worn out, or that their mission in 3-D has finished and they are being recalled to join the Masters on the higher planes. In either case, the person submits gladly to the process and looks forward to meeting old friends again.

As death approaches, the person spends more and more time in meditation. They recall life's lessons and their reaction to them. They search for any attachment to thoughts and desires connected with the 3-D realm, and release those attachments. As they contemplate this lifetime they will start to feel if the path of return is there for them, and they will start to do the work to construct the next body that they will inhabit. They will bend their will to constructing the most perfect physical body that they will need to learn the lessons of the next lifetime; they will imprint on that body all the knowledge of the mysteries that they have learnt in this lifetime.

They tread, through meditation, the path that they will walk when they take their last breath, the process listed above. They will know where they are going and, understanding the process, will walk the path unmolested by any being so that they may end up in the Ashram of their Master.

They recognize that their approaching death is not a separation from their Loved ones, quite the opposite. They know that once they leave the physical body they will be able to connect to their loved ones in a more powerful way, to know their hopes and fears and to guide them through those. In this lifetime they have connected to the deeper aspect of every person they have met, and as such, that imprint will accompany them on their journey undisturbed.

When the spiritual person feels the time has come where death is approaching, they gather around themselves the friends they have done spiritual work with in this lifetime. Those that cannot be there in the physical, they ask to be there in essence. They also summon around them all the Beings of Light that have supported them in their spiritual work in this lifetime and ask them to wait for them on the threshold.

I recommend that no more than seven people are needed to hold a space around the bedside as the person prepares to leave. As I mentioned above, it is important the kind of space that is created around a person when they take their last breath. For a spiritual person, music can be played which holds a special significance for that person, and will raise their consciousness to connect to the Divine. The lighting in the room should be predominantly orange, as this greatly enhances the separation of the Etheric body from the physical shell. There should be a candle burning, so that anything that is released in the process of taking the last breath will jump to the flame and be consumed. Again, in Alice Bailey, Djwhal Khul recommends that Sandalwood as a perfume should be burnt to facilitate the separation of the Etheric body. The Master that I associate with the death and dying process is of course Djwhal Khul who is the Tibetan Master, and of course the Tibetans hold the tradition of death and dying. Another recommendation is that Aura Soma sprays can be used around the room and over the bed of the dying person. The obvious choice would be the Djwhal Khul spray.

As the time approaches, the person's friends in the room describe a circle of protection around the space. They summon the Four Mighty Archangels of the four quadrants to stand in those places. They sit in silent meditation as their friend takes their last breath; for those with eyes to see, as the door swings open, they see a Mighty One come forth to welcome their comrade. There is a shift in the space, like a slight breeze passing through the room, and their friend is gone.

It is said that one who does the work will pass through the gates of death in full consciousness, and for their friends who have accompanied them to the door, they will also see the path that they will walk in some future time.

So how do we do a healing for a person who is dying? Well, as we have said above, it is all about attachment. As we have said, by being with the person in the space for three days prior to them taking their last breath, we can do all in our power to help them connect to the people they need to in order to say their last goodbyes. However, we can also help them through healing.

The kind of healing I have always done is to help that person, through sympathetic resonance, to sever all ties to people, places, or events in that lifetime. This can be done by summoning in the energies of the Archangel Michael, or any other cosmic force which provides a clearing of karmic connections.

We thank, on behalf of the person, the body in which they find themselves, for the service it has done to allow that person to learn the lessons of the 3-D realm.

We contact the Soul of that person and connect it to their consciousness so that it may direct them in the journey they are about to take.

We summon the Angels that guide beings through death, these being the Archangel Azrael, the archetypal forces of Anpu (Anubis), Tehuti (Thoth), Amenta, Hades, Persephone, etc. We also call on that person's Guardian Angel, which has guided them throughout that lifetime.

Such is the power of the service that we can do that I relate the experience I had when I did this for my stepfather when he died. He had died in the hospice in which I had worked, and I had done the work for him as I have described above. However, because of the connection to the physical body which can still be there for three days after taking the last breath, it is vital that we do the healing for those three days. It was, then, that I found myself in the funeral parlour where his body was interred. It was the second day after his death that I had been there to do this service. I did the meditation/healing and as it completed, to my astonishment, I saw him lift out of the physical shell, but what was more extraordinary was that I perceived two other deceased people in the back of the funeral parlour who also left with him.

We have discussed above that this process of seven days of abstraction from the physical form applies to any living thing. The process that we are in at the moment is that the being that we know as Gaia is now abstracting herself from her physical form, which is this third dimensional planet. She is undergoing the process of travelling through her Underworld to be reborn on the fourth dimensional plane. What happens in death to any other being is happening to Gaia. If you think about it, and look at what is happening in the world we are definitely in the process. If you observe any person who is dying what happens to the physical body? It starts to deteriorate, it starts to show signs of wear, it starts to show signs of falling apart. You only have to look around to see this process in the world at this time.

Not so long ago I read in a newspaper that the Amazon rainforest was known as the lungs of the world. Now it has been re-categorised as one of the worst polluters of the world because of all the destruction of trees by burning. It is one of the worst sources of the hothouse gases which are affecting the weather at this time. It does not take a great jump in consciousness to see the analogy with the disease of the lungs in a human being. What sign is that when the lungs of the world have become bronchitic?

My feeling is, and I have to stress that this is only my opinion, that we are in the three-day process leading up to death, to the last breath of Gaia on the third dimensional plane. In 2012, that magical date is when Gaia will take her last breath on the physical plane. Then for the next three days there will be dissolution of Gaia from the third dimensional plane. I also have to point out here that a day in the life of a planet is not a day as we perceive it. It encompasses a much vaster period of time as we conceive it. It is therefore that I leave the speculation of how long that may be to you.

Again, my feeling is, just as it is the truth for a human being, the body that Gaia will inhabit already exists on the higher dimensional planes. All of the species that appear to have become extinct are now inhabitants on that planet, as are many of the human race who have left recently due to natural and created disasters.

Just as a human being takes seven days to transit to higher dimension, so Gaia is undergoing the same process. I feel that this is what the ascension is truly about. Ascension is about leaving behind an old vehicle, it falls into dissolution, and you are reborn in another vehicle on a higher dimension. It does not strike me, therefore, that the 3rd dimensional Earth is going to be reborn. How can it? We all know that we are transiting into a higher dimension. So this focus on cleansing the Earth, on cleansing this and cleansing that, it's pointless because what is happening is just a natural process. The Earth as a third dimensional being is dying. It is."

Angelic Reiki

The Gift of Healing through Death

At the beginning of this chapter, I described how the state of consciousness that someone is in when they take their last breath colours and creates the environment in which they will find themselves on the astral plane. The chakra from which they will exit their consciousness from the body is also dictated by how they are feeling at the time of death. To guide, feel and support someone through the deathing process is probably the profoundest gift that we can give to anyone. It is also a wonderful gift to the person who is supporting them. When death is understood, there is no reason why it cannot be celebrated with great joy. Also the opening of the dimensional gate which facilitates the transition brings a beautiful gift to everyone who is present.

Kevin's story of his grandmother's death illustrates the profound gift that healing at this time can bring. His grandmother had lived a very ordinary life. She had no religious or spiritual interest; her life had simply involved work and family. Because all of her focus had been on the mundane material plane her consciousness, was destined to leave her physical body through the solar plexus. This would have meant that after the transition she would have created exactly the same reality on the astral plane and reincarnated at some time probably into a very similar reality. Kevin spent the full seven days with her. He spent much of the time in meditation in the way that he has described earlier in this chapter. When it came to her last breath, he actually saw her leave through the crown chakra. Most people spend a lifetime of spiritual work in order to attain a level of consciousness that will allow them to leave the body as an Ascended Master through the crown chakra. Ever since her death in the early '90s, she was around Kevin as one of his guides.

There is no greater gift that we can give and it is so simple.

The Seven Step Process for Healing through Death

Step one/completion. The days leading up to someone's last breath are a time for completion. Do everything you can in a practical way to enable them to do this. Follow what seems important to them. It may be simply paying a bill or spending time with a relative or friend. If it is important to them then it is a step toward completion. In the days and weeks leading up to the last breath, people are often very open to forgive and forget old wounds. Enabling someone to do this is a great service. It is worthwhile gently encouraging them to do this. Do everything practically possible to enable them to connect with family and friends, especially those that they may not have seen for some time and some completion of forgiveness needs to take place. It may be that they want to talk about part of their life, so just being a good listener is all that is needed. Any karma that is not worked out will hang over to the next lifetime.

Step two/letting go of hopes and wishes. Part of the completion process is encouraging the person to let go. It may be that they cannot complete certain things in this lifetime, so encouragement and reassurance that enable them to let go of the desire is of great support. Examples are that they may have always wanted to write a book or travel to Australia etc. Many people find it difficult to let go of their Loved ones because they perceive (and this is a very powerful erroneous idea that is perpetuated) that they will be separated from the ones that they Love after they have taken the last breath. They will not. They will still feel a connection to everyone they know. They are simply dropping the physical body and not going anywhere. Yes the ones still in incarnation will feel the grief of separation of the presence, physically, of the person. I am not suggesting that one hides one's grief or pretends that is going to be okay, but we can reassure the person who is leaving the incarnation that we will be alright and that they will reunite with other friends and family, perhaps even Masters and Angels, once they have left the incarnation. People often see '*dead*' relatives during the few days leading up to their departure. These are real and have come to collect them. It will always be someone who they have had a deep connection with in the past. Reassure the person who is dying that they will not be alone.

Step three/surrounding them in Love. Hold the space of Love and support around the person who is leaving the incarnation. How they feel just before will be how they feel when their breath is no longer in the body. Children usually deal very well with someone who is dying and can often bring joy and playfulness to the bedside. Yes, they will grieve if someone close dies, but it has been shown that they cope better if they have had contact with the person and understand and share in the process.

Step four/the room. There are certain practical things that enable an easy transition into spirits. These are flowers in the room, incense, especially frankincense, a candle, orange tinted light, homoeopathic remedies and flower essences.

Step five/prayer, healing and meditation. One does not have to have been attuned to a healing system in order to be able to work with the Angels and Masters. Simply asking for their presence will cause them to be there. Call in whatever energy or being most resonates with you. Don't doubt that they will be there whether you feel them or not. Archangel Michael is often invoked as he is the Angel that cuts ties with the past. Djwhal Khul is the Master most associated with the death in process. He brings Love and healing and often accompanies those who have connected with him as they transit into spirit. Other beings that can be invoked are Sokar the Egyptian god of new cycles or Anubis who accompanies the dead. Just sitting in meditation creates a very good space. If you have not meditated before, don't worry, just sit still and peacefully and feel Love in the whole space around you. It is important to speak lovingly about the person. Even though they may seem to be in a coma because their ability to hear is very acute and they will register conversations that are held around them.

Step six/releasing the physical body. The physical body has the consciousness and part of the struggle in the few days before someone takes their last breath can be the unwillingness of the diva of the body to let go of the person who has inhabited that body for so long. Simply thanking the physical body, the intelligence and consciousness of that body can be of great help. Ask Archangel Michael to lovingly cut all ties between the person and their physical body. Remember they are not their physical body and never have been. It has simply been a vehicle. It is best to touch the physical body as little as possible after the last breath as this can anchor the connection back to the physical again.

Step seven/releasing the spirit. The actual extraction of the person from the physical body takes seven days with the fourth day being the one on which they take the last breath. The fact that the person has stopped breathing does not mean that they have disconnected in consciousness from the physical body. In the UK we are fortunate in that we often have time after the day of the last breath to be with the person; simply continuing to hold the loving space and asking for helpers, guides and Angels to support them on their way.

Those Left Behind

There is a grieving process and it is important to knowledge and embrace this and not push it to one side. I believe it is also important to get support during this time. As an incarnated personality we miss the human contact. Any belief that we have lost this person or that they have gone somewhere unnecessarily increases the sense of loss. This belief also makes it more difficult and sometimes impossible for the person who has left their physical body to make contact with us. Knowing that they have not gone anywhere and that they have simply released physicality and that they remain around us as a consciousness makes it possible for them to relate to us. This can happen in a number of ways. You may feel a light tingling or a sensation as if a feather is touching you. They may also create signs that they are around. The most frequent signs that Kevin uses are car number plates and feathers. When I rented a car about three months after he had died, the man processing my rental agreement did not just pass me some keys and tell me where to find the car. For some reason, he hesitated and then said that he knew which car I needed to have. He went out of the office to find this car and when he brought it to me I noticed that the number plate virtually spelled KEV 1 N. Just the other day, when I went out to sit on the balcony of our bedroom, right in the middle of Kevin's chair there was a feather. Every time that I lose sight that he is still here and get caught up in the emotions of missing him, he sends me a message. I might get an e-mail from the most unexpected people telling me that Kevin had given them a message for me. One, for example, was from a Greek guy who I had never met. We will not get these messages or understand the signs if we believe that the person who has died is not around us anymore.

Chapter Twelve
The Invocation of Angels for Specific Purposes

In the chapter about Angels I talked about the Angelic name being an energy formula and that it is by sounding the name that energy is created around wherever you are. It is important to sound the name in a very particular way. The vowels need to be emphasised and the name sounded with the intention that it fills the space and actually vibrates every molecule and atom of that space. With this intention this really happens and the energy of that space changes as does yours. The sound vibrates in your consciousness around you and tunes it into the special purpose of that Angel. This is how a uniting of our energy and the energy of the Angel occurs. The Angelic consciousness merges with our consciousness imprinting its Divine perfection into our very being. It is our perception of Angels as separate beings with a specific identity that has limited and restricted their potent and transformative power. The idea of an Angel as a being in its own right limits the potential to use this aspect of creation in its most potent form. The projection of Angels as beings with wings, with opinions and agendas, is disempowering and untrue.

Here is a list of Archangels that can be used for specific purposes.

Archangel Metatron—supports the creation of any new project.

Archangel Michael—mm-EE-kII-eLL—brings anything to completion ready for the start of a new beginning.

Archangel Sandalphon—supports a new project manifesting.

Christine Core

Archangel Raphiel—raa-f-I-EEll—brings balance to any situation by shining a light on whatever needs to be seen.

Archangel Gabriel—g-aa-brEE-ell—brings re-birth and new beginnings.

In the following list are seventy-two Angel names and their gifts. These are otherwise known as the seventy names of Metatron. Each group of eight is associated with one of the Sephiroth, or circles, on The Tree of Life starting from the top with a Sephiroth known as Kether(chapter five). The last one, Malkuth, associated with the Archangels Sandalphon, does not have a group of Angels. It is the grounding of the creative energy of the divine into 3 D manifestation. The required supported energy of any of these Angels can be called in at any time but they also have a specific affinity to a period of five days. For example these dates are given as *3/26-30, the 3 denoting March, with the numbers 26 to 30, the days*. It is particularly powerful and supportive to invoke the angelic energy on these particular days and, as with astrology, the information indicates the energy that accompanies those particular dates. It can also be interesting to link your birthday with a particular angelic energy and see what you personally may be working with.

Each of these seventy-two Angels holds a specific archetype, and by sounding the name we can bring that energy into our consciousness and use it to help us. They are also associated with a period of five days. Although it is only part of the picture, you can see which Angelic energy you were born with, and I have also listed a couple of famous people who were born with that Angelic energy. These energies can be viewed in the same way as astrological signs in that there is the positive and negative aspect, each one reflecting the lessons learnt and the lessons not learnt. You will see that some of the famous people came to learn a lesson and others used the energy in a positive and fulfilling way.

Although some of these Angels have a particular affinity for healing, we do not call them in specifically by name for an Angelic Reiki healing. The healing Angel that is present for a healing will bring exactly what is needed. Our intervention is not required. It is only the egoic self who identifies with being a healer that can have an opinion and want to influence the healing. In Angelic Reiki the job of the healer is to give everything over to

Angelic Reiki

the Angelic Kingdom of Light without prejudice or opinion. Our mantra is that as human personalities there is only one thing we know and that is that we don't know.

There is no reason why more than one Angel cannot be used to bring a combination of energies.

The Gifts of Seventy-Two Angels

Example: **Vehuiah**—name of the Angel. (vay-HOO-ee-YAH) is the phonetic pronunciation. 3/21-26; March 21st to 26th is the five-day period of this Angels influence. Johann Sebastian Bach and Elton John; famous people born during that period. See if you can see the Angelic qualities in these people. It may also represent lessons to be learnt. You can use these to look at your own lessons and qualities or to call in the Angelic energy for the day. This is a wonderful way to start each day.

1. **Vehuiah**—(vay-HOO-ee-YAH). Helps receive enlightenment and to expand the consciousness. The Angel Vehuiah allows us to see the highest perception of the principles that rule everything and the wisdom to use them. 3/21-26. Johann Sebastian Bach and Elton John.

2. **Jeliel**—(JAY_lee_EL). This Angel of Love and wisdom allows us to use these higher gifts to overcome difficulties and experience Divine perfection on the physical plane. It energises the creation of new beginnings through balancing the masculine and feminine. 3/26-30. Vincent Van Gogh and Eric Clapton.

3. **Sitael**—(SIT-AH-EL). Through the principles that constructed the universe this Angel supports us in building anything that is based on truth and Love. It also helps us to recognise anything that is not built on truth. 3/31-4. Sir Alec Guinness and Doris Day.

4. **Elemiah**—(eh-LEEM-ee-YAH). This Angel connects us to the power of the Divine and enables us to see and remove anything, both personal and external, that may compromise us understanding the Divine plan. 4/5-9. Vivienne Westwood and Butch Cassidy.

5. Mahasiah—(mAh-HA-see-YAH). Helps live in peace with all. If any mistakes have been made, this Angel cancels any disharmony that may be caused bringing everything back into peace and balance. Influences learning. 4/10-14. Omar Sharif and Al Green.

6. **Lelahel**—(LAY-la-HEEL). This Angel brings light and understanding to any situation or idea. It also brings light for healing and speeds recovery. It will also put you in the lime light so that your new ideas and projects will be seen. Influences the sciences. 4/15-20. Leonardo Da Vinci, Charles Chaplin and Kevin Core.

7. **Achaiah**—(a-KA-hee-YAH). This is the Angel of patience and communication and has a specific influence on industry. Through sharing information it brings all of the cogs into synchronization. Helps discover natural secrets. 4/21-25. William Shakespeare and Oliver Cromwel.

8. **Cahetel**—(KA-heh-TEL). This Angel of Divine blessings brings nurturance and new growth. It also has a relationship with fertility having an affinity with nature and agriculture. It brings a healing balm to past hurts. 4/26-30. Ferrucio Lamborghini and Duke Ellington.

9. **Aziel**—(AA-ze-EL). The Angel of forgiveness. This Angel brings a spontaneous feeling of Love and forgiveness for oneself and others. Forgiveness is always the herald of new beginnings. It also helps us to keep promises and renew friendship with sincerity and faith. 5/1-5. Karl Marx and Mary Astor.

10. **Aladiah**—(a—LA-dee-YAH). This Angel of grace brings the ability to let go of dogmatic views and rigidly held principles. In this way it also supports the reintegration of an individual back into a group when beliefs and dogma has separated them. 5/6-10. Orson Welles and Harry S. Truman.

11. **Lauviah**—(LOW-vee-YAH). This Angel of victory sustains us through difficult times and also helps when two people are going through a difficult time. It also brings success. Lauviah is also said to protect against lightning. 5/11-15. George Lucas and Salvador Dali.

Angelic Reiki

12. **Hahaiah**—(ha-HA-ee-YAH). This is the Angel of refuge and shelter. It helps find an inner place of peace and will also protect from outside dangers. Because of its relationship with inner work it can help us discover the mystery of dreams. 5/16-20. Dame Margot Fonteyn and Pope John Paul II.

13. **Yezalel**—(Iye-za-LEL). The influence is on the internal and external worlds. Through bringing truth and loyalty we find a deeper relationship with the self. The quality of faithfulness and loyalty create fruitful relationships on every level and brings reconciliation. 5/21-25. Alexander Pope and Joan Collins.

14. **Mebahel**—(MAY-BA-HEL). This is the Angel of truth, liberty and justice. It does affect the relationship with ourselves but also has an important influence over the legal profession and the law. It protects and helps against those wishing to usurp our power. Influences and protects truth. 5/26-31 John F. Kennedy and George Formby.

15. **Hariel**—(HA-ree-EL). As the Angel of purification it sweeps away any blocks to a deeper connection with the higherself. On a very practical level it supports the physical body in recognising which foods cause congestion and toxicity. It also clears away anything that may inhibit our creativity. It supports painters and poets. 6/1-5. Marilyn Monroe and Henry Kissinger.

16. **Hakamiah**—(HA-ka-mee—YAH). These energies of loyalty and faithfulness help us stay true to our own inner beliefs whatever influences may come or whatever someone else may say and think. Helps us to never betray our own truth and supports victory over enemies, internal and external. 6/6-10. Alexander Pushkin and Frank Lloyd Wright.

17. **Laviah**—(LAH-vee-YAH). If there is anything that is not understood, the sounding of this Angels name will bring the answer. This may be a spiritual concept, a part of one self, or a message in a dream. There is a sadness that comes when there is a battle between living a spiritual life or one of materially based values. This is often part of the spiritual path. Laviah helps us to put aside material desires and addiction and instead

Christine Core

helps us participate in creative pursuits like art, poetry and music. 6/11-15. Richard Strauss and W.B.Yeats.

18. **Caliel**—(KA-lee-EL). As Angel of Divine Justice it allows us to see that our most vociferous judge, jury and prosecutor is ourselves. Through Love this Angel quiets the self-critic that often clouds our view of our own true value and the value of what we are doing. 6/16-21. Enoch Powell and Sir Paul McCartney.

19. **Leuviah**—(LOO-vee-YAH). Our bad or painful memories are often stronger than joyful and positive ones. Through expanded intelligence Leuviah enables us to reap all memories as valuable and important information. It also enables us to link into the Akashic Records. 6/22-26. Lord Louis Mountbatten and George Orwell.

20. **Pahaliah**—(pa-HA-lee-YAH). This is the Angel of redemption. Redemption has two meanings; to get the value of something back and to be delivered from bondage. Pahaliah works on the emotions allowing us to claim the understanding and wisdom that our emotions hide us from. We find our true value and are freed from the bondage of lower emotions. 6/27-7/1. Captain James Cook, King Henry VIII and Diana Princess of Wales.

21. **Nelchael**—(NEL-ka-EL). When we feel tired of the search for answers and the pursuit of new knowledge the Angel Nelchael renews our desire for learning. This is not just restricted to spiritual knowledge. This energy would also help a student prepare for exams especially mathematics and geometry. 7/2-6. George Walker Bush, Elizabeth Emmanuel and Nancy Davis Reagan.

22. **Yeiaiel**—(IAY-ah-YEL). Fame and renown are double-edged swords. For those who seek fame for its own sake it is hollow and egotistical. Others resist fame and are afraid of standing out in the crowd. The Angel Yeiaiel brings the courage and skills to be seen and successful, smoothing the sea of emotions that can unbalance fame and fortune. It also supports success in business trips.7/7-11. Pierre Cardin, Geiorgio Armani and Ringo Starr.

23. **Melahel**—(MAY-la-HEEL). Through a connection to nature and natural things the Angel Melahel brings living in peace without war. It also connects us to the healing potential of plants and supports healers who work in this way. This Angel has an affinity for the elements of Earth, water and air. 7/12-6. Rembrandt and Emily Pankhurst.

24. **Hahuiah**—((ha-HOO-ee-YAH). This is the Angel of protection through truth. How often do we wrongly accuse ourselves of failure in some way and forget the truth that we had done our best at the time. The Angel Hahuiah also allows the truth to come to the surface when someone has been wrongly accused. It is a powerful support in the freeing of dissidents and exiles. 7/17-22. W.G.Grace and Paul Von Reuter.

25. **Nith-Haiah**—(NIT-ha-YAH). This is the Angel of spiritual wisdom and spiritual magic. It helps us to understand and appreciate the cycles of creation and its mysteries. 7/23-27. George Bernard Shaw and Mick Jagger.

26. **Haaiah**—(HA-ee-YAH). Through its affinity with political science and ambition this Angel brings integrity to politicians, ambassadors and diplomats so that their decisions can reflect Divine logic and reason. It also brings openness and truthfulness when parties come together to sign the political treaties. 7/28-8/1. Arnold Schwarzenegger and Henry Ford.

27. **Yerathel**—(YEH-ra-TEEL). This Angel's blessing is the gift known as the propagation of light. It supports all those who bring liberty and justice. It includes Love and peace into the writings and words of politicians. It disperses the energies of impulsive thoughts that may lead someone to respond to unjust provocation, accusation and attack. 8/2-6. Barack Obama and Miriam Rothschild.

28. **Seheiah**—(say-HAY-ee-YAH). This Angel is specifically for healing and its particular quality is longevity. It brings a balance between the mind and emotions. It is also said that the Angel Seheiah will protect against lightning and accidents. 8/7-12. Ralph Bunche (Nobel Peace Prize) and Herbert Hoover.

Christine Core

29. **Reiyel**—(RAY-ee-YEEL). Liberation is a quality that this Angel brings. It enables us to let go of old belief systems and traditions. It also supports us in releasing our attachment to material objects and pleasures. It will support the ascension process. 8 /13-17. Alfred Hitchcock and James Cameron.

30. **Omael**—(O-ma-EEL). The essence of this Angel is fertility and multiplicity. This energy affects every level of growth whether it be spiritual growth or planting seeds in our garden. It brings support and abundance to new projects. The energy is enhanced when it is invoked at the time of the waxing moon. 8/18-22. Gene Roddenberry and Bill Clinton.

31. **Lecabel**—(LAY-ka-BEEL). This Angel has a strong affinity with the mind, supporting all intellectual challenges and problem solving. It also quiets emotions that can cloud clear thinking. 8/23-28. William Wilberforce and Robert Walpole.

32. **Vasariah**—(va-SAH-ree-YAH). Only with grace and compassion can we truly forgive both ourselves and others. This Angel allows us to embrace the energy of clemency bringing a balanced perspective to be taken whenever judgement of others may come up. It is a beautiful energy for anyone who is involved as a lawyer or arbitrator in any way. 8/29-9/2. Richard Attenborough and Michael Jackson.

33. **Yehuiah**—(Yyay-HOO-see-YAH). This is the Angel of subordination to higher orders. If feelings of betrayal arise then the answer lies within ourselves and we need to ask in what way we had betrayed our own higher self's or Soul's guidance. This is the Angel that brings the energy of "Not My Will But Thy Will". 9/3-7. Queen Elizabeth I and Jesse James.

34. **Lehahiah**—(lay-HA-hee-YAH). This Angel brings obedience and is similar to the previous Angel in that it supports us in patiently following our true path. It also brings obedience to truth to all those in authority. 9/8-12. D.H Lawrence and Christopher Columbus.

35. **Chevakiah**—(cha-VA-kee-YAH). This is the Angel of reconciliation. On a personal level it supports self forgiveness. It also helps unite family

members especially if there is dispute over family financial affairs or a will. 9/13-17. J.B Priestley and Agatha Christie.

36. **Menadel**—(MEH-na-DEEL). This is a very grounding Angel and its special attributes affect our inner and outer world. In the outer world it supports maintaining high ethics in the workplace and in our inner world it supports us in continuing the work we need to do. 9/18-23. Brian Epstein and Stephen King.

37. **Aniel**—(AH-nee-EL). This is the Angel that breaks cycles. When we seem to be stuck and repeatedly attracting the same karma this Angel will help us see the pattern and break free of it. It also has an affinity with the cycles of nature. 9/24-28. T.S Eliot and William Faulkner.

38. **Haamiah**—(ha-AH-mee-YAH). This is the Angel of ritual and ceremony and can be invoked for social celebrations like birthdays and weddings or during spiritual ceremonies. It allows all energies that are invoked to flow through with grace and gentle transformation. 9/29-10/3. Mahatma Ghandi and. Julie Andrews

39. **Rehael**—(RAY-ha-EL). This is a very important energy that could be of great value today. It governs the relationship between children and their parents. This Angel can be invoked to bring healing in families experiencing divorce. It can also create a better relationship between adult children and their elderly parents. 10/4-8. Bob Geldof and Vladimir Putin.

40. **Yeiazel**—(YAY-ah-ZEL). This Angel brings healing balm when we are going through difficult times. It is the Angel of Divine consolation and comfort. It also has an affinity for communication and will support writers having their manuscripts accepted by a publisher. 10/9-13. Nana Mouskouri and Marie Osmond.

41. **Hahahel**—(HA-ha-HEL). The energy of this Angel is mission. It allows us to understand our own personal mission and for us to follow it with purposefulness and Love. It also brings peace to those who feel driven by their mission. 10/14-18. Dwight D. Eisenhower and Lennox Lewis.

Christine Core

42. Mikael—(MI-ka-EEL). This is the Angel that covers political authority and order. It supports the integration of higher principles into the minds and hearts of all those who assume a position of authority both in the political field and in the area and law enforcement and military. 10/19-23. Alfred Nobel and Peter Mandelson.

43. Veuliah—(vay-OO-lee-AH). This is the Angel of prosperity. It also allows us to see what true wealth is and appreciate the true value of what we have. Oscar Wilde said that most people know the price of everything and the value of nothing. 10/24-28. Pablo Picasso and Theodore(Teddy) Roosevelt.

44. Yelahiah—(Yay-LAH-hee-YAH). This Angel brings the energies of the karmic warrior. If you feel tired of the lessons that life presents this Angel will bring courage and endurance supporting us in overcoming old karma in a positive way. It also encourages travel as a way of learning as this reflects the inner journey of dissolving karmic debt and acquiring new wisdom. 10/29-11/2. Charles Atlas and L.S. Lowry.

45. Sealiah—(say-HA-lee-YAH). This Angel brings motivation and willingness. It has an affinity with fire energy. This is fire in the belly which keeps us going and fire in the heart that allows us to do it with Love. It also brings the warmth to nurture new plants. 11/3-7. Scott Joplin and Madame Curie.

46. Ariel—(AH-ree-EL). The Archangel Ariel helps reveal what we don't understand. Through dreams, signs and symbols, it will bring us clues and clarity. 11/8-12. Martin Luther and Richard Burton.

47. Asaliah—(a-SA-lee-YAH). This Angel brings the gift of contemplation. We can receive clarity and wisdom when we sit quietly and get in touch with our inner knowing. Sitting in contemplation awakens and integrates our sensitivity. This can facilitate us to be more aware of what is on other people's minds.11/13-17. Claude Monet and Sir Magdi Yacoub.

48. Mihael—(MIH-a-EL). This is the Archangel of fertility and fruitfulness. These qualities support both the planting of the seed of an idea and supporting it right through to its fruition. It also brings together the male and the female which are needed for new birth and propagation. 11/18-22. Meg Ryan and Edwin Hubble.

49. Vehuel—(VAY-hoo-EL). This is the Angel of elevation and grandeur. The words, written by Marianne Williamson and used by Nelson Mandela in his inaugural speech express the gifts of this Angel most beautifully; "Our deepest fear is not that we are inadequate. Our deepest fear is that we are powerful beyond measure. It is our light, not our darkness, that most frightens us. We ask ourselves, who am I to be brilliant, gorgeous, talented, and fabulous? Actually, who are you not to be? You are a child of God. Your playing small doesn't serve the world. There's nothing enlightened about shrinking so that other people won't feel insecure around you. We are all meant to shine, as children do. We are born to make manifest the glory of God that is within us. It's not just in some of us, it's in everyone. And as we let our own light shine, we unconsciously give other people permission to do the same. As we are liberated from our own fear, our presence automatically liberates others." 11/23-27. Billy Connolly and Tina Turner.

50. Daniel—(DA-nee-EL). This is the Angel of eloquence connecting our thoughts and words to the clarity and honesty of Divine intervention. Invoking this energy will support spiritual teachers and anyone wishing to communicate spiritual ideas. 11/28-12/2. Sir Winston Churchill and Woody Allen.

51. Hahasiah—(HA-ha-si-YAH). This is the energy of the 'Philosopher's Stone'; the wisdom of the universe as healing medicine. Invoking this energy will help anyone who is doing research into new medicines especially if it is from a natural source like herbs or crystals. 12/3-7. Walt Disney and Thomas Barnado.

52. Imamiah—(ee-MA-mee-YAH). Healing modalities like N.L.P. allow us to re-frame our past so that any limiting beliefs and experiences can be transmuted and be replaced by thoughts and feelings that will bring a positive outcome in the future. This Angel creates and supports this process. 12/8-12. Alexander Solzhenitsyn and Frank Sinatra.

Christine Core

53. Nanael—(NA-na-EL). This is the Angel of Spiritual communication and helps us understand esoteric information. It brings deeper states of meditation and receiving messages, ideas and wisdom from spirit. 12/13-16. Nostradamus and Ludwig Van Beethoven.

54. **Nithael**—(NIT-ha-EL). This is the Angel to which we all want to connect. It brings rejuvenation and eternal youth. When we live in line with our purpose and harmony and Love flows freely through our words and deeds, we are connected to the source of eternal life. 12/17-21. Betty Grable and Edith Piaf.

55. **Mebahiah**—(Me-BA-hee-YAH). We need intellectual abilities but our society today has allowed the intellect to overrule the heart and our connection to Divine wisdom. This Angel fills our thoughts with Love, truth and clarity and supports us in connecting to the Divine mind. 12/22-26. Mao Tse-Tung and Giacomo Puccini.

56. **Poiel**—(Poi-YEL). This Angel supports synchronicity. This sometimes presents itself as good fortune. It also supports us in using what we are given wisely and in a way that can be understood and of value to others. 12/27-31. Louis Pasteur and Marlene Dietrich.

57. **Nemmamiah**—(ne-MA-mee-YAH). This is the Angel of discernment. This is a very valuable attribute so that we can respond appropriately to situations and information. 1/1-5. J Edgar Hoover and J.R.R. Tolkien.

58. **Yeialel**—(YAY-a-LEL). When we use the power of the mind to observe our responses to situations, we can become a Master of our emotions. This Angel supports the mental discipline in order to do this. 1/6-10. Professor Stephen Hawking and Richard Nixon.

59. **Harakel**—(HA-ra-HEL). This is the Angel of intellectual richness. Spiritual knowledge is real abundance. This Angel also supports us in using our intellectual abilities to create financial riches as well. 1/11-15. Aristotle Onassis and Margaret Beckett.

60. **Mitzrael**—(MITS-ra-EL). This Angel supports the connection and communication between our soul and incarnated self. It also brings

knowledge and wisdom to the healing of psychological diseases. 1/16-20. Muhammad Ali and Paul Cezanne.

61. **Umabel**—(OO-ma-BEL). This Angel brings the ability and an understanding of the importance of working with groups. These may be Angelic or Ascended Masters or collaboration with friends and associates. It also allows us to realise that we are connected to everything and helps reveal the secrets of the natural world. It also supports the bringing together of like-minded people who can work towards a shared goal. This is very much the energy that we are in during the Ascension process. 1/21-25. Christian Dior and Sir Francis Bacon.

62. **Iah-Hel**—(EE-a-HEL). When you put a call out to the universe for some understanding or information, this is the perfect Angel to support you. It also helps with receiving wisdom whilst sat in quiet meditation. 1/26-30. Wolfgang Amadeus Mozart and Lewis Carroll.

63. **Anianuel**—(a-NA-oo-EL). This is the Angel that unites us and breaks through all barriers of race and culture. It also brings communication and unity between the inner self and the outside world. It also quells emotions that create separation. 1/31-2/4. Boris Yeltsin and Felix Mendelssohn.

64. **Mehiel**—(MAY-hee-EL). Sometimes we need passion, commitment and determination to bring to fruition what we desire to create. This Angel also brings the help needed to fulfil a project, especially for those involved in communication through literature and philosophy. 2/5-9. Bob Marley and Zsa Zsa Gabor.

65. **Damabiah**—(da-MA-bee-YAH). This Angel brings a fountain of wisdom connecting us to Divine wisdom so that we can use this in our every day lives. 2/10-14. Sir Vivian Fuchs and Lord Randolph Churchill.

66. **Manakel**—(MA-na-KEL). Our heads can have lots of opinions and judgements but our heart knows the truth. This Angel brings the discernment so that we can understand whether an idea or venture is a good idea or not. It also helps us to recognise the clues when something negative is in our path. There are people and things that can be described as evil in the world today that use tactics to dis-empower us and create fear.

This Angel will allow us to see the truth and to be able to clearly distinguish between good and evil. 2/15-19. John McEnroe and Yoko Ono.

67. **Eyael**—(AY-ya-EL). We can study and learn spiritual truths but we need to be able to ground these and apply them in everyday life. This Angel supports us in doing this. 2/20-24. George Washington and Lord Baden Powell.

68. **Xabuiah**—(X-ha-BU-hee-YAH). This Angel supports healing by allowing us to connect to nature and quieten internal turmoil. 2/25-29. Rabbi Julia Neuberger and Elizabeth Taylor.

69. **Rochel**—(ro-SHEEL). If we have latent talents and abilities, some of which may have been learnt in a past life, this Angel supports in calling these forwards so that we can use them again. It also helps us to find anything that we think we may have lost. 3/1-5. Frederic Chopin and Alexander Graham Bell.

70. **Jabamiah**—(ya-BA-mee-YAH). This is the Angel of alchemy and transformation. Alchemy is not just about transmuting base metals into gold. It is also the ability to transform how we see the world and recognising the golden opportunities and Divine nature of everything around us. This Angel brings us internal alchemy and transformation which is then reflected in the world around us. 3/6-10. Michelangelo and Yuri Gagarin.

71. **Haiyael**—(HA-ee-ya-EL). This Angel is the Divine warrior. The image is very similar to the Archangel Michael as Haiyael also has a sword and shield. Sometimes in spiritual work we need warrior energy in order to see us through difficult times. This is the courageous hero who finds truth and peace. 3/11-15. Malcolm Campbell and Percival Lowell.

72. **Mumiah**—(MOO-mee-YAH). As the last Angel in this cycle, Mumiah brings completion, endings and the foundations for rebirth. Everything is in cycles and until we totally complete the cycle that we are in we cannot claim its fruits and benefits as the foundation for the next cycle. This Angel allows us to see the gifts in the difficulties and challenges that have occurred so that we can create a new beginning. 3/16-20. Rudolf Nureyev and Dr. Livingstone.

Resources

The following can be found on the Angelic Reiki International website (www.angelicreikimagic.com):

Free MP3 meditations to download.

- Kevin Core facilitating a cleansing by the Archangel Metatron.
- Kevin Core facilitating an attunement to the seventy-two names of The Archangel Metatron
- Kevin Core leading the ancient Pentagram ritual connecting to the Archangels of the four directions.

Three live recordings of transformational meditations facilitated by Christine Core

- Cleansing limiting beliefs
- Feel and know yourself as the greater consciousness that you are.
- A journey into your future receiving a *'vision'* of you and the earth after 2012 and beyond.

Shop

Five Unique healing CDs

- Experience an Angelic Reiki healing with Kevin.
- The Soul Integration Meditation.
- Connecting to the Ten Archangels of the Tree of Life through colour.

- Karmic clearing facilitated by Kevin and the Archangel Michael.
- Deep physical cleansing.

Cards.

- Reproduction of the only four remaining magical symbols for Archangels.
- Pentagram cards for the elements and Archangels of the four directions.

Information on courses

Statement of the codes of ethics

Links to regional Angelic Reiki websites worldwide

Extensive list of Q & A

Links the Christine Core's other web-sites

Sources

"Esoteric Healing", Alice Bailey: Lucis Press

"A Dictionary of Angel", Gustaff Davidson: Free Press

"Birth Angel", Terah Cox: Andrew: McMeel Publishing

"A Return to Love", Marianne Williamson: HarperCollins

About the Author

Christine Core is the co-founder of Angelic Reiki. From the original channelling of the system in 2002/3 by Kevin Core until his death in 2009, Kevin and Christine taught, and lived together in sacred relationship bringing a balance of the male and female to their work. Kevin still guides and works with her and everyone connected to Angelic Reiki. From his Love filled place in Spirit he will bless everyone who connects through this book, if they so wish.

Christine has devoted her life fully to the healing arts since training as a professional homeopath in 1987. Her ten years running a healing centre in the United Kingdom and practicing as a full-time homeopath have given her a deep understanding of the healing process and spiritual path. In 2001, she felt it was time for a change of direction and bought an around-the-world air ticket and travelled independently for fifteen months. This journey brought remarkable experiences and adventures in many countries including New Zealand, Japan, Borneo and Southeast Asia.

Christine now lives at the foot of the Valley of Kings near Luxor, Egypt where she and Kevin made their home in 2005. She continues to travel worldwide teaching Angelic Reiki (it is now represented in over twenty-three countries) plus two other workshops: "The Golden Heart Merkabah of Creation" and "New Shamballa" which they created together. These are also Angelic in essence underpinning and deepening an understanding of the *Law* of creation; living in freedom empowered through LOVE. These three workshops Angelic Reiki, Golden Heart Merkabah of Creation and New Shamballa constitute the three pillars of service, wisdom and personal power.

Christine can be contacted through these websites:

www.angelicreikimagic.com
www.magicmerkabahangel.com
www.newshamballa.com

Printed in Great Britain
by Amazon